HARRAP'S

German Vocabulary

Compiled by
LEXUS
with
Horst Kopleck

HARRAP
London

First published in Great Britain 1988
by HARRAP BOOKS Ltd
19–23 Ludgate Hill London EC4M 7PD

© *Harrap Books Limited* 1988

Reprinted 1988 and 1989

ISBN 0-245-54630-8

Printed in Great Britain by
Richard Clay Ltd, Bungay, Suffolk

INTRODUCTION

This German vocabulary book has been compiled to meet the needs of those who are learning German and is particularly useful for those taking the GCSE examinations. The basic vocabulary required for this exam is fully treated in this book.

A total of over 6,000 vocabulary items divided into 65 subject areas gives a wealth of material for vocabulary building, with the words and phrases listed being totally relevant to modern German. The majority of vocabulary items are listed in thematic groupings within each section, thus enabling the user to develop a good mastery of the relevant topic.

An index of approximately 2,000 words has been built up with specific reference to GCSE exam requirements. This index is given in English with cross-references to the section of the book where the German vocabulary item is given.

This book will be an invaluable tool for success in German.

Abbreviations used in the text:

m	masculine
f	feminine
n	neuter
pl	plural
gen	genitive
dat	dative
acc	accusative
R	registered trade mark

CONTENTS

1. Describing People
2. Clothes and Fashion
3. Hair and Make-Up
4. The Human Body
5. How Are You Feeling?
6. Health, Illnesses and Disabilities
7. Movements and Gestures
8. Identity
9. Age
10. Jobs and Work
11. Character and Behaviour
12. Emotions
13. The Senses
14. Likes and Dislikes
15. Daily Routine and Sleep
16. Food
17. Housework
18. Shopping
19. Sport

CONTENTS

20. Leisure and Hobbies

21. The Media

22. Evenings Out

23. My Room

24. The House

25. The City

26. Cars

27. Nature

28. What's the Weather Like?

29. Family and Friends

30. School and Education

31. Money

32. Topical Issues

33. Politics

34. Communicating

35. Letter Writing

36. The Phone

37. Greetings and Polite Phrases

38. Planning a Holiday and Customs Formalities

39. Railways

40. Flying

41. Public Transport

42. At the Hotel

CONTENTS

43. Camping, Caravanning and Youth Hostels
44. At the Seaside
45. Geographical Terms
46. Countries, Continents and Place Names
47. Nationalities
48. Languages
49. Holidays in Germany
50. Incidents
51. Accidents
52. Disasters
53. Crimes
54. Adventures and Dreams
55. The Time
56. The Week
57. The Year
58. The Date
59. Numbers
60. Quantities
61. Describing Things
62. Colours
63. Materials
64. Directions
65. Abbreviations

1. BESCHREIBUNG VON MENSCHEN
DESCRIBING PEOPLE

sein	to be
haben	to have
aussehen	to look
scheinen	to seem
wiegen	to weigh
beschreiben	to describe
ziemlich	quite, rather
sehr	very
zu	too
die Beschreibung	description
die Erscheinung	appearance
das Aussehen	look
die Haltung	bearing
die Größe	height, size
das Gewicht	weight
das Geschlecht	sex
das Haar	hair
der Bart	beard
der Schnurrbart	moustache
Augen (*pl*)	eyes
die Haut	skin
der Teint	complexion
ein Pickel (*m*)	spot, pimple
ein Leberfleck (*m*)	mole, beauty spot
Sommersprossen (*pl*)	freckles
Falten (*pl*)	wrinkles
Grübchen (*pl*)	dimples
eine Brille	glasses
jung	young
alt	old
groß	tall
klein	small, short

mittelgroß	of average height
dick	fat
fettleibig	obese
dünn	thin, skinny
schlank	thin, slim
muskulös	muscular
gebrechlich	frail-looking
schön	beautiful, good-looking (*woman*)
gutaussehend	good-looking, handsome
hübsch	pretty
häßlich	ugly
pickelig	spotty
sonnengebräunt	sun-tanned
braungebrannt	tanned
blaß	pale
faltig	wrinkled
er/sie hat ... Augen	he/she has ... eyes
blaue	blue
grüne	green
graue	grey
braune	brown
hellbraune	hazel
schwarze	black
graublaue	grey-blue
graugrüne	grey-green

wie ist er/sie?
what's he/she like?

können Sie ihn/sie beschreiben?
can you describe him/her?

ich bin 1 Meter 75 groß
I'm 1.75 metres (5 feet 9 inches) tall

ich wiege 70 Kilo
I weigh 70 kilos (11 stone)

ein Mann mittlerer Größe
a man of medium height

er benimmt sich eigenartig
he behaves strangely

er sieht etwas seltsam aus
he looks a bit strange

See also Sections **2 CLOTHES, 3 HAIR AND MAKE-UP, 4 BODY** *and* **61 DESCRIBING THINGS**.

2. KLEIDUNG UND MODE
CLOTHES AND FASHION

sich anziehen	to dress
sich ausziehen	to undress
anziehen	to put on
ausziehen	to take off
anprobieren	to try on
tragen	to wear
anhaben	to have on
passen	to suit, to fit

Kleider   clothes

ein Mantel (*m*)	coat, overcoat
ein Regenmantel (*m*)	raincoat
ein Anorak (*m*)	anorak
ein Blouson (*n*)	bomber jacket, blouson
eine Jacke	jacket
ein Sakko (*n*)	(sports) jacket
ein Anzug (*m*)	suit
ein Kostüm (*n*)	lady's suit
ein Smoking (*m*)	dinner jacket
eine Uniform	uniform
eine Hose	trousers
eine Skihose	ski pants
eine Jeans	jeans
Blue-Jeans (*pl*)	jeans
eine Latzhose	dungarees
ein Trainingsanzug (*m*)	tracksuit
die Shorts (*pl*)	shorts
ein Kleid (*n*)	dress
ein Abendkleid (*n*)	evening dress
ein Rock (*m*)	skirt
ein Minirock (*m*)	mini-skirt

ein Pullover (*m*)	jumper, sweater
ein Pulli (*m*)	pullover
ein Rollkragenpullover (*m*)	polo neck (jumper)
eine Weste	waistcoat
eine Jacke	cardigan
ein Hemd (*n*)	shirt
eine Bluse	blouse
ein Nachthemd (*n*)	nightdress
ein Schlafanzug (*m*)	pyjamas
ein Pyjama (*m*)	pyjamas
ein Bademantel (*m*)	dressing gown
ein Morgenrock (*m*)	dressing gown (*for women*)
ein Bikini (*m*)	bikini
ein Badeanzug (*m*)	swimming costume
die Unterwäsche	underwear
ein Höschen (*n*)	panties
ein Büstenhalter (*m*)	bra
ein BH (*m*)	bra
ein Unterhemd (*n*)	vest
eine Unterhose	(under)pants
ein T-Shirt (*n*)	T-shirt
ein Unterrock (*m*)	underskirt, petticoat
Strumpfhalter (*pl*)	suspenders
Strümpfe (*pl*)	stockings
die Strumpfhose	tights
Socken (*pl*)	socks
Kniestrümpfe	knee-length socks
Wollstrümpfe	woollen socks
Baumwollstrümpfe	cotton socks

Schuhe   shoes

Schuhe (*pl*)	shoes
Stiefel (*pl*)	boots
Gummistiefel	Wellington boots
Turnschuhe	trainers, gym shoes
Skistiefel	ski boots
Sandalen (*pl*)	sandals

Hausschuhe	slippers
ein Paar	a pair of
die Sohle	sole
der Absatz	heel
flache Absätze	flat heels
Bleistiftabsätze	stiletto heels

Zubehör   accessories

ein Hut (*m*)	hat
ein Strohhut (*m*)	straw hat
ein Sonnenhut (*m*)	sun hat
eine Haube	bonnet
eine Mütze	cap
eine Kappe	cap
ein Schal (*m*)	scarf
ein Kopftuch (*n*)	(head)scarf
Handschuhe (*pl*)	gloves
Fausthandschuhe (*pl*)	mittens
eine Krawatte	tie
ein Schlips (*m*)	tie
eine Fliege	bow tie
Hosenträger (*pl*)	braces
ein Gürtel (*m*)	belt
der Kragen	collar
ein Knopf (*m*)	button
Manschettenknöpfe (*pl*)	cufflinks
ein Reißverschluß (*m*)	zip
Schnürsenkel (*pl*)	shoelaces
ein Band (*n*)	ribbon
ein Taschentuch (*n*)	handkerchief
ein Regenschirm (*m*)	umbrella
eine Handtasche	handbag

Schmuck

jewellery

ein Juwel (*n*)	jewel
das Silber	silver
das Gold	gold
ein Edelstein (*m*)	precious stone
eine Perle	pearl
ein Diamant (*m*)	diamond
ein Smaragd (*m*)	emerald
ein Rubin (*m*)	ruby
ein Saphir (*m*)	sapphire
ein Ring (*m*)	ring
Ohrringe (*pl*)	earrings
ein Armband (*n*)	bracelet
ein Armreif (*m*)	bangle
eine Brosche	brooch
eine Halskette	necklace
eine Kette	chain
ein Anhänger (*m*)	pendant
eine Armbanduhr	watch
ein Perlenkollier (*n*)	pearl necklace

Größe

size

klein	small
mittelgroß	medium
groß	large
kurz	short
lang	long
weit	wide, loose-fitting
eng	tight
die Größe	size
die Taille	waist
die Schuhgröße	shoe size
die Kragenweite	collar size
die Hüftweite	hip measurement
die Oberweite	bust/chest measurement

die Taillenweite	waist measurement

Stil — style

das Modell	model
die Farbe	colour
die Schattierung	shade
das Muster	pattern, design
uni	plain
bedruckt	printed
bestickt	embroidered
kariert	check(ed)
geblümt	flowered, flowery
gepunktet	with polka-dots, spotted
gestreift	striped
schick	elegant, smart
elegant	elegant
formell	formal
lässig	casual
sportlich	snazzy
schlampig	sloppy
einfach	simple, plain
knallig	loud, gaudy
modisch	fashionable
altmodisch	old-fashioned
maßgeschneidert	made-to-measure
dekolletiert	low-cut, low-necked

Mode — fashion

die (Winter)kollektion	(winter) collection
die Herrenmode	men's fashions
die Herrenkonfektion	menswear
die Damenmode	ladies' fashions
die Damenkonfektion	ladies' wear
die Modebranche	clothing industry
die Schneiderei	dressmaking

Kleider von der Stange	off-the-peg clothes
die Haute Couture	haute couture, high fashion
ein(e) Schneider(in)	dressmaker
ein(e) Modeschöpfer(in)	fashion designer
das Mannequin	fashion model
ein Dressman (*m*)	male model
eine Modenschau	fashion show

es ist aus Leder
it's (made of) leather

sie hat ein blaues Kleid an
she has a blue dress on

ich möchte gern etwas Preiswerteres
I'd like something cheaper

ich möchte einen zu diesem Hemd passenden Rock
I'd like a skirt matching this shirt

kann ich die Hose anprobieren?
can I try these trousers on?

welche Größe/Schuhgröße haben Sie?
what is your size/shoe size?

rot steht mir nicht
red doesn't suit me

diese Hose steht Ihnen gut
these trousers suit you

ich muß mich erst noch umziehen
I have to get changed first

See also Sections **14 LIKES AND DISLIKES, 18 SHOPPING, 62 COLOURS** *and* **63 MATERIALS.**

3. HAARE UND MAKE-UP
HAIR AND MAKE-UP

kämmen	to comb
bürsten	to brush
schneiden	to cut
nachschneiden	to trim
sich frisieren	to do one's hair
sich (*dat*) (**die Haare**) **kämmen**	to comb one's hair
sich (*dat*) **die Haare bürsten**	to brush one's hair
sich (*dat*) **die Haare färben**	to dye one's hair
blondieren	to bleach
sich (*dat*) **die Haare schneiden lassen**	to have a hair-cut
sich (*dat*) **die Haare färben lassen**	to have one's hair dyed
sich (*dat*) **die Haare fönen lassen**	to have a blow-dry
sich im Spiegel betrachten	to look at oneself in the mirror
sich schminken	to put one's make-up on
sich parfümieren	to put on perfume
sich (*dat*) **die Fingernägel lackieren**	to paint one's nails
sich rasieren	to shave

Haarlänge
hair length

... Haare haben	to have ... hair
kurze	short
lange	long
mittellange	medium-length
eine Glatze haben	to be bald

Haarfarbe

hair colour

. . . Haare haben	to have . . . hair
blonde	blonde/fair
braune	brown
schwarze	black
rote	red/ginger
graue	grey
graumelierte	greying
weiße	white
blond sein	to be blonde/fair-haired

Frisuren

hairstyles

. . . Haar haben	to have . . . hair
krauses	curly
gewelltes	wavy
glattes	straight
dichtes	thick
gefärbtes	dyed
fettiges	greasy
trockenes	dry
der (Haar)schnitt	(hair-)cut
eine Dauerwelle	perm
eine Locke	curl
der Scheitel	parting
Strähnchen (*pl*)	highlights, streaks
ein Pony (*m*)	fringe
ein Pferdeschwanz (*m*)	pony tail
ein Zopf (*m*)	braid, plait, pigtail
ein Kamm (*m*)	comb
eine Haarbürste	hairbrush
eine Haarspange	hairslide
eine Haarnadel	hairpin
ein Lockenwickler (*m*)	roller, curler
ein Lockenstab (*m*)	tongs
eine Perücke	wig

das (Haar)shampoo	shampoo
das Haarwaschmittel	shampoo
das Gel	gel
das Haarspray	hair spray
die Schuppen (*pl*)	dandruff

Make-up

make-up

die Schönheit	beauty
die Gesichtscreme	face cream
die Feuchtigkeitscreme	moisturizing cream
die Gesichtspackung	face pack
das Puder	powder
die Puderdose	compact
die Grundierungscreme	foundation cream
der Lippenstift	lipstick
die Wimperntusche	mascara
der Lidschatten	eye-shadow
der Nagellack	nail varnish
der Make-up-Entferner	make-up remover
der Nagellackentferner	nail varnish remover
das Parfüm	perfume
das Toilettenwasser	toilet water, eau de toilette
das Eau de Cologne	cologne
das Kölnisch Wasser	cologne
der Deodorant	deodorant
das Deospray	deodorant

Rasur

shaving

der Bart	beard
der Schnurrbart	moustache
das Rasiermesser	razor
der Rasierapparat	shaver
der Elektrorasierer	electric shaver
die Rasierklinge	razor blade
der Rasierpinsel	shaving brush
die Rasiercreme	shaving foam
das Rasierwasser	aftershave

4. DER KÖRPER
THE HUMAN BODY

Körperteile	parts of the body
der Kopf	head
der Hals	neck
die Kehle	throat
der Nacken	nape of the neck
die Schulter	shoulder
die Brust	chest, bust
der Busen	bust
Brüste (*pl*)	breasts
der Bauch	stomach
der Rücken	back
der Arm	arm
der Ell(en)bogen	elbow
die Hand	hand
das Handgelenk	wrist
die Faust	fist
der Finger	finger
der Daumen	thumb
der Zeigefinger	index finger
der Mittelfinger	middle finger
der Ringfinger	ring finger
der kleine Finger	little finger
der Nagel	nail
die Taille	waist
die Hüfte	hip
der Hintern	behind, bottom
das Gesäß	buttocks
das Bein	leg
der Schenkel	thigh
das Knie	knee
die Wade	calf
der Knöchel	ankle
der Fuß	foot

die Ferse	heel
die Zehe	toe
ein Organ (*n*)	organ
ein Glied (*n*)	limb
ein Muskel (*m*)	muscle
ein Knochen (*m*)	bone
das Skelett	skeleton
das Rückgrat	spine
die Wirbelsäule	spinal column
eine Rippe	rib
das Fleisch	flesh
die Haut	skin
das Herz	heart
die Lunge	lungs
das Verdauungssystem	digestive tract
der Magen	stomach
die Leber	liver
Nieren (*pl*)	kidneys
die Blase	bladder
das Blut	blood
die Ader	vein
die Vene	vein
die Arterie	artery

der Kopf   the head

der Schädel	skull
das Gehirn	brain
das Haar	hair
das Gesicht	face
Gesichtszüge (*pl*)	features
die Stirn	forehead
Augenbrauen (*pl*)	eyebrows
Wimpern (*pl*)	eyelashes
das Auge	eye
(Augen)lider (*pl*)	eyelids
die Pupille	pupil
die Nase	nose
das Nasenloch	nostril

die Backe	cheek
die Wange	cheek
der Backenknochen	cheekbone
die Schläfe	temple
der Kiefer	jaw
der Mund	mouth
Lippen (*pl*)	lips
die Zunge	tongue
ein Zahn (*m*)	tooth
ein Milchzahn (*m*)	milk tooth
ein Weisheitszahn (*m*)	wisdom tooth
das Kinn	chin
das Doppelkinn	double chin
ein Grübchen (*n*)	dimple
das Ohr	ear
das Ohrläppchen	ear lobe

See also Sections **6 HEALTH** *and* **7 MOVEMENTS AND GESTURES**.

5. WIE GEHT ES IHNEN?
HOW ARE YOU FEELING?

sich fühlen	to feel
werden	to become
hungrig	hungry
durstig	thirsty
satt	full
schläfrig	sleepy
fit	fit, on form
in Hochform	very fit, on top form
müde	tired
erschöpft	exhausted
atemlos	out of breath
träge	lethargic
stark	strong
schwach	weak
gebrechlich	frail
gesund	in good health
bei guter Gesundheit	healthy, in good health
krank	sick, ill
wach	awake, alert
erregt	agitated
im Halbschlaf	half asleep
durchnäßt	soaked
durch(ge)froren	frozen
zu	too
völlig	totally

er ist müde
he is/feels tired

er sieht müde aus
he looks tired

er schläft
he is asleep

ich fühle mich schwach
I feel weak

mir ist nicht wohl
I don't feel well

was hast du?
what's wrong?

mir ist (zu) warm/kalt
I'm (too) hot/cold

ich habe Hunger/Durst
I'm hungry/thirsty

ich sterbe vor Hunger!
I'm starving!

mir reicht's
I've had enough

ich bin am Ende meiner Kräfte
I'm worn out

See also Section **6 HEALTH**.

6. GESUNDHEIT, KRANKHEITEN UND BEHINDERUNGEN
HEALTH, ILLNESSES AND DISABILITIES

gesund sein	to be well
krank sein	to be ill
krank werden	to fall ill
bekommen	to catch
Magenschmerzen (*pl*)	stomach ache
Kopfschmerzen (*pl*)	headache
Halsschmerzen (*pl*)	sore throat
Rückenschmerzen (*pl*)	backache
Zahnschmerzen (*pl*)	toothache
sich krank fühlen	to feel sick
seekrank sein	to be seasick
Schmerzen haben	to be in pain
leiden an (+*dat*)	to suffer from
erkältet sein	to have a cold
ein Herzleiden (*n*) **haben**	to have a heart condition
sich (*dat*) **den Arm/das Bein brechen**	to break one's leg/arm
sich (*dat*) **den Knöchel verstauchen**	to sprain one's ankle
sich an der Hand verletzen	to hurt one's hand
verletzen	to hurt
bluten	to bleed
weh tun	to hurt
erbrechen	to vomit
husten	to cough
niesen	to sneeze
schwitzen	to sweat
zittern	to shake, to shiver
Fieber haben	to have a temperature
in Ohnmacht fallen	to faint
ohnmächtig sein	to be in a coma

rückfällig werden	to have a relapse
behandeln	to treat
pflegen	to nurse, to tend
sich kümmern um	to look after
rufen	to call
kommen lassen	to send for
sich anmelden	to make an appointment
untersuchen	to examine
raten	to advise
verschreiben	to prescribe
operieren	to operate
operiert werden	to have an operation
sich die Mandeln entfernen lassen	to have one's tonsils taken out
röntgen	to X-ray
verbinden	to dress (*wound*)
brauchen	to need
einnehmen	to take
einreiben	to rub in
sich ausruhen	to rest
heilen	to heal, to cure
sich erholen	to recover
eine Diät machen	to be on a diet
abnehmen	to lose weight
zunehmen	to put on weight
sich verschlimmern	to get worse
sterben	to die
krank	ill, sick
unwohl	unwell
schwach	weak
geheilt	cured
bei guter Gesundheit	in good health
fit	fit
lebendig	alive
schwanger	pregnant
allergisch gegen	allergic to
anämisch	anaemic
epileptisch	epileptic

diabetisch	diabetic
verstopft	constipated
betrunken	drunk
schmerzhaft	painful, sore
ansteckend	contagious
ernst	serious
schlimm	bad
infiziert	infected
geschwollen	swollen
gebrochen	broken
verstaucht	sprained

Krankheiten   illnesses

eine Krankheit	disease
ein Leiden (*n*)	disease
der Schmerz	pain
eine Epidemie	epidemic
ein Anfall (*m*)	fit, attack
eine Wunde	wound
eine Verstauchung	sprain
ein Bruch (*m*)	fracture
eine Blutung	haemorrhage, bleeding
das Fieber	fever, temperature
der Schluckauf	hiccups
der Husten	cough, coughing
der Schock	shock
der Puls	pulse
die Temperatur	temperature
die Atmung	respiration, breathing
die Blutgruppe	blood group
der Blutdruck	blood pressure
die Regel	period
ein Abszeß (*m*)	abscess
eine Abtreibung	abortion
Aids	Aids
eine Angina	angina
die Arthritis	arthritis
das Asthma	asthma

eine **Blasenentzündung**	cystitis
die **Blinddarmentzündung**	appendicitis
die **Bronchitis**	bronchitis
der **Durchfall**	diarrhoea
die **Epilepsie**	epilepsy
eine **Erkältung**	cold
eine **Fehlgeburt**	miscarriage
eine **Gehirnerschütterung**	concussion
ein **Geschwür** (*n*)	ulcer
die **Grippe**	flu
ein **Herzinfarkt** (*m*)	heart attack
das **Heufieber**	hay fever
eine **Infektion**	infection
der **Keuchhusten**	whooping cough
die **Kinderlähmung**	polio
das **Kopfweh**	headache
der **Krebs**	cancer
ein **Leistenbruch** (*m*)	hernia
die **Leukämie**	leukemia
eine **Lungenentzündung**	pneumonia
eine **Magenverstimmung**	upset stomach, indigestion
die **Masern** (*pl*)	measles
die **Migräne**	migraine
der **Mumps**	mumps
ein **Nervenzusammenbruch** (*m*)	nervous breakdown
die **Pocken** (*pl*)	smallpox
das **Rheuma**	rheumatism
der **Rheumatismus**	rheumatism
die **Röteln** (*pl*)	German measles
ein **Schnupfen** (*m*)	cold
ein **Sonnenstich** (*m*)	sunstroke
die **Tollwut**	rabies
die **Tuberkulose**	TB
der **Typhus**	typhoid
die **Verstopfung**	constipation
die **Windpocken** (*pl*)	chickenpox

Hautverletzungen   skin complaints

eine **Verbrennung**	burn

eine Schnittverletzung	cut
ein Kratzer (m)	scratch
ein Insektenstich (m)	insect bite
ein Jucken (n)	itch
ein Ausschlag (m)	rash
die Akne	acne
Pickel (pl)	spots
Krampfadern (pl)	varicose veins
eine Warze	wart
ein Hühnerauge (n)	corn
eine Blase	blister
ein blauer Fleck	bruise
eine Narbe	scar
ein Sonnenbrand (m)	sunburn

Behandlung — treatment

die Medizin	medicine
die Hygiene	hygiene
die Gesundheit	health
die Empfängnisverhütung	contraception
die Behandlung	(course of) treatment
die Erste Hilfe	first aid
ein Krankenhaus (n)	hospital
eine Klinik	clinic
ein Kurort (m)	spa, health resort
die Sprechstunde	surgery hours
das Wartezimmer	waiting room
das Sprechzimmer	(doctor's) surgery
ein Notfall (m)	emergency
ein Krankenwagen (m)	ambulance
eine Trage	stretcher
die Watte	cotton wool
ein Pflaster (n)	plaster
ein Verband (m)	bandage, dressing
eine Armbinde	sling
ein Gipsverband (m)	plastercast
das Heftpflaster	sticking plaster
eine Damenbinde	sanitary towel

ein Tampon (*n*)	tampon
Krücken (*pl*)	crutches
eine Operation	operation
die Narkose	anaesthetic
eine Bluttransfusion	blood transfusion
eine Röntgenaufnahme	X-ray
die Diät	diet
eine Kur	health cure
der Krankenschein	medical card
die Krankenkasse	health insurance scheme
die Beratung	consultation
ein Termin (*m*)	appointment
ein Rezept (*n*)	prescription
die Genesung	convalescence
ein Rückfall (*m*)	relapse
die Erholung	recovery
der Tod	death
der Arzt	doctor
die Ärztin	woman doctor
der diensthabende Arzt	duty doctor
ein Spezialist (*m*)	specialist
eine Krankenschwester	nurse
ein Pfleger (*m*)	male nurse
ein Kranker, eine Kranke	sick person
ein(e) Patient(in)	patient

Medikamente   medicines

das Medikament	medicine
eine Apotheke	(dispensing) chemist's
eine Drogerie	chemist's
die Antibiotika (*pl*)	antibiotics
ein Schmerzmittel (*n*)	painkiller
eine Kopfschmerztablette	aspirin
ein Beruhigungsmittel (*n*)	tranquillizer
eine Schlaftablette	sleeping pill
ein Abführmittel (*n*)	laxative
ein Stärkungsmittel (*n*)	tonic

Vitamine (*pl*)	vitamins
der Hustensaft	cough mixture
eine Tablette	tablet
die Pille	the pill
die Tropfen (*pl*)	drops
ein Antiseptikum (*n*)	antiseptic
die Salbe	ointment
eine Spritze	injection
die Impfung	vaccination

beim Zahnarzt

at the dentist's

ein Zahnarzt (*m*)	dentist
eine Plombe	filling
ein Gebiß (*n*)	dentures
der Zahnersatz	dentures
die Karies	caries
der Zahnbelag	plaque

Behinderungen

disabilities

behindert	disabled
körperbehindert	physically disabled
geistig behindert	mentally handicapped
mongoloid	suffering from Down's syndrome
blind	blind
einäugig	one-eyed
farbenblind	colour-blind
kurzsichtig	short-sighted
weitsichtig	long-sighted
schwerhörig	hard of hearing
taub	deaf
taubstumm	deaf and dumb
gelähmt	crippled, lame
ein Behinderter, eine Behinderte	handicapped person, disabled person
ein geistig Behinderter	mentally handicapped person

ein Blinder, eine Blinde	blind person
ein Stock (*m*)	stick
ein Rollstuhl (*m*)	wheelchair
ein Hörgerät (*n*)	hearing aid
eine Brille	glasses
Kontaktlinsen (*pl*)	contact lenses

was fehlt Ihnen?
what's wrong with you?

wie fühlen Sie sich?
how are you feeling?

ich fühle mich nicht sehr gut
I don't feel very well

mir ist schlecht/schwindlig
I feel sick/dizzy

wo tut es weh?
where does it hurt?

es ist nichts Ernstes
it's nothing serious

gute Besserung!
get well soon!

es geht mir heute schon viel besser
I'm feeling a lot better today

ich habe Fieber gemessen
I took my temperature

er hat 38 Fieber
he's got a temperature of 101

sie ist an den Augen operiert worden
she had an eye operation

haben Sie etwas gegen ...?
have you got anything for ...?

See also Section **4 BODY.**

7. BEWEGUNGEN UND GESTEN
MOVEMENTS AND GESTURES

Kommen und Gehen	coming and going
anhalten	to stop
ankommen	to arrive
auf und ab gehen	to pace up and down
auftauchen	to turn up
ausrutschen	to slip
aussteigen aus	to get off (*train, bus etc*)
bleiben	to stay, to remain
davoneilen	to rush away
einsteigen in (*+acc*)	to get on (*train, bus etc*)
erscheinen	to appear
folgen	to follow
gehen	to go, to walk
gehen durch	to go through
herauskommen aus	to come out of
hereinkommen in (*+acc*)	to come in(to)
hereinstürzen	to rush in
herunterkommen	to come down(stairs)
hinaufgehen	to go up(stairs)
hinausgehen aus	to go out of
hineingehen in (*+acc*)	to go in(to)
hinuntergehen	to go down(stairs)
holen gehen	to go and get, to fetch
humpeln	to limp
hüpfen	to hop
kommen	to come
laufen	to run
losgehen	to set off
näherkommen	to come near
rasen	to belt along
rennen	to run
rückwärts gehen	to walk backwards
schleichen	to slide

schreiten	to stride
sich ausruhen	to rest
sich beeilen	to hurry
sich (*dat*) die Beine vertreten	to go for a stroll
sich hinlegen	to lie down
sich verstecken	to hide
spazierengehen	to go for a walk
springen	to jump
stolpern	to trip
taumeln	to stagger
trödeln	to dawdle
überqueren	to cross
verschwinden	to disappear
vorbeigehen	to pass, to go past
weggehen	to go away
weitergehen	to continue, to go on
wie angewurzelt dastehen	to be rooted to the spot
wiederkommen	to return, to come back
zu/ins Bett gehen	to go to bed
zurückgehen	to go back (in/home)
zurückkommen	to come back (in/home)
die Ankunft	arrival
die Abreise	departure
der Anfang	beginning
der Beginn	beginning
das Ende	end
der Eingang	entrance
der Ausgang	exit, way out
die Rückkehr	return
die Überquerung	crossing
ein Spaziergang	walk, stroll
die Gangart	way of walking
ein Schritt (*m*)	step
eine Pause	rest
der Sprung	jump
Schritt für Schritt	step by step
im Schrittempo	at walking speed
mit langsamen/schnellen Schritten	at a slow/fast pace

Handlungen

actions

Handlungen	actions
anfangen	to start
auffahren	to give a start, to jump
aufhören	to stop
aufmachen	to open
aufstehen	to get/stand up
beenden	to finish
beginnen	to begin
berühren	to touch
bewegen	to move
drücken	to push, to squeeze
entfernen	to remove
fallenlassen	to drop
fangen	to catch
festhalten	to hold tight
halten	to hold
herunterlassen	to lower
hochheben	to lift, to raise
legen	to put
nehmen	to take
öffnen	to open
schließen	to close
setzen	to put, to place
sich ausruhen	to (have a) rest
sich ausstrecken	to stretch out
sich bücken	to stoop
sich hinhocken	to squat down
sich hinknien	to kneel down
sich hinlegen	to lie down
sich hinsetzen	to sit down
sich lehnen (gegen/auf)	to lean (against/on)
sich lehnen (über)	to lean (over)
sich umdrehen	to turn round
stellen	to put
stoßen	to hit, to knock
verschließen	to close, to lock
verstecken	to hide
werfen	to throw

ziehen	to pull, to drag
zumachen	to shut

Haltung

postures

kauernd	squatting
hingehockt	squatting
kniend	kneeling
auf Knien	on one's knees
liegend	lying down
ausgestreckt	lying stretched out
gelehnt (auf/gegen)	leaning (on/against)
auf allen vieren	on all fours
sitzend	sitting, seated
stehend	standing
angelehnt	leaning
hängend	hanging
regungslos	motionless

Gesten

gestures

treten	to kick
boxen	to punch
schlagen	to slap
beißen	to bite
das Gesicht verziehen	to make a face
ein Zeichen (n) geben	to make a sign
ein Handzeichen (n) geben	to signal with one's hand
die Stirn runzeln	to frown
die Schultern zucken	to shrug (one's shoulders)
mit den Achseln zucken	to shrug (one's shoulders)
nicken	to nod
blicken	to glance
einen Blick werfen	to cast a glance
aufblicken	to look up, to raise one's eyes
die Augen senken	to look down, to lower one's eyes
blinzeln	to blink
zwinkern	to wink

zeigen auf (+*acc*)	to point at
lachen	to laugh
den Kopf schütteln	to shake one's head
lächeln	to smile
lachen	to laugh
grinsen	to grin
gähnen	to yawn
ein Achselzucken (*n*)	shrug
eine Bewegung	movement
ein Blick (*m*)	look, glance
ein Gähnen (*n*)	yawn
eine Geste	gesture
eine Grimasse	grimace
ein Grinsen (*n*)	grin
ein Kopfschütteln (*n*)	shake of the head
ein Lächeln (*n*)	smile
das Lachen	laugh
ein Nicken (*n*)	nod
ein Schlag (*m*)	punch, blow
ein Schulterzucken (*n*)	shrug
ein Tritt (*m*)	kick
ein Zeichen (*n*)	sign, signal, gesture
ein Zwinkern (*n*)	wink

wir sind mit dem Auto hingefahren
we went there by car

ich gehe zu Fuß zur Schule
I walk to school

er lief nach unten
he ran downstairs

ich rannte hinaus
I ran out

sie rannte über die Straße
she ran across the street

er kommt morgen zurück
he'll be back tomorrow

8. IDENTITÄT
IDENTITY

Name   name

nennen	to name, to call
taufen	to christen
sich nennen	to call oneself
heißen	to be called
unterschreiben	to sign
buchstabieren	to spell
die Identität	identity
die Unterschrift	signature
der Name	name
der Familienname	family name
der Nachname	surname
der Zuname	surname
der Vorname	first name
der Mädchenname	maiden name
der Spitzname	nickname
der Geburtsort	place of birth
die Staatsangehörigkeit	nationality
die Initialen (*pl*)	initials
Herr Martin	Mr Martin
Frau Müller	Mrs Müller
Fräulein (Frl.) Schröder	Miss Schröder
Herren	gentlemen
Damen	ladies

Geschlecht   sex

eine Frau	woman
eine Dame	lady
ein Mädchen (*n*)	girl
ein Mann (*m*)	man

ein Herr (m)	gentleman
ein Junge (m)	boy
männlich	masculine, male
weiblich	feminine, female

Familienstand   marital status

geboren werden	to be born
sterben	to die
heiraten	to marry
sich verloben	to get engaged
sich scheiden lassen	to get divorced
die Verlobung lösen	to break off one's engagement
ledig	single
unverheiratet	unmarried
verheiratet	married
verlobt	engaged
geschieden	divorced
getrennt lebend	separated
verwitwet	widowed
verwaist	orphaned
ein Junggeselle (m)	bachelor
eine Junggesellin	unmarried woman
eine alte Jungfer	old maid, spinster
der Ehemann	husband
die Ehefrau	wife
der Mann	husband
die Frau	wife
der Exmann	ex-husband
die Exfrau	ex-wife
der Verlobte	fiancé
die Verlobte	fiancée
der Bräutigam	bridegroom
die Braut	bride
ein Paar (n)	couple
die Jungverheirateten (pl)	newly-weds
ein Witwer (m)	widower

eine Witwe	widow
ein Waisenkind (*n*)	orphan
eine Waise	orphan (*male and female*)
die Zeremonie	ceremony
die Geburt	birth
die Taufe	christening
der Tod	death
die Beerdigung	funeral
die Hochzeit	wedding
die Verlobung	engagement
die Scheidung	divorce

Adresse   address

leben	to live
wohnen	to live (*in a place*)
mieten	to rent
vermieten	to let
sich (*dat*) **eine Wohnung teilen**	to share a flat
die Adresse	address
der Wohnort	place of residence
die Etage	floor, storey
die Postleitzahl	postcode
die (Haus)nummer	number
die Telefonnummer	phone number
das Telefonbuch	telephone directory
der Hauswirt	owner, landlord
der Vermieter	landlord
der Mieter	tenant
der Nachbar	neighbour
bei Klaus	at Klaus's
in der Stadt	in town
am Stadtrand	in the suburbs
auf dem Lande	in the country

Religion   religion

katholisch	Catholic

protestantisch	Protestant
evangelisch	Protestant
anglikanisch	Anglican
moslemisch	Muslim
jüdisch	Jewish
atheistisch	atheist

wie heißt du/heißen Sie?
what is your name?

ich heiße Paul Schmidt
my name is Paul Schmidt

wie heißt du/heißen Sie mit Vornamen?
what is your first name?

er heißt Rainer
his name is Rainer

wie schreibt man das?
how do you spell that?

wie schreiben Sie sich?
how do you spell/write your name?

wo wohnst du/wohnen Sie?
where do you live?

ich wohne in Köln/in Österreich
I live in Cologne/in Austria

es ist im dritten Stock
it's on the third floor

ich wohne (in der) Stephanstraße (Nummer) 27
I live at 27, Stephanstraße

ich wohne seit einem Jahr hier
I've been living here for a year

See also Section **29 FAMILY AND FRIENDS.**

9. ALTER
AGE

jung	young
alt	old
das Alter	age
die Geburt	birth
das Leben	life
die Jugend	youth
die Jugendzeit	adolescence
das Alter	old age
das Geburtsdatum	date of birth
der Geburtstag	birthday
ein Baby (*n*)	baby
ein Kind (*n*)	child
ein Teenager (*m*)	teenager
ein Erwachsener (*m*)	adult
ein Jugendlicher (*m*)	young person
junge Leute	young people
eine junge Frau	young woman
ein junges Mädchen	young girl
ein junger Mann	young man
eine alte Frau	old woman
eine ältere Dame	elderly woman
ein alter Mann	old man
ein älterer Herr	elderly man
alte Leute	old people
die Alten (*pl*)	the old

wie alt bist du/sind Sie?
how old are you?

ich bin 20 Jahre (alt)
I'm 20 years old

wann bist du geboren?
when were you born?

am ersten März 1960
on the first of March 1960

in welchem Jahr sind Sie geboren?
what year were you born in?

ich bin 1968 in Stuttgart geboren
I was born in Stuttgart in 1968

ein einen Monat altes Baby
a one-month old baby

ein achtjähriges Kind
an eight year old child

ein sechzehnjähriges Mädchen
a sixteen year old girl

eine Frau von dreißig Jahren
a woman of thirty

mit 20
at the age of 20

ein Mann mittleren Alters
a middle-aged man

ein Herr im reiferen Alter
an elderly gentleman

10. ARBEIT UND BERUF
JOBS AND WORK

arbeiten	to work
vorhaben	to intend
werden	to become
sich interessieren für	to be interested in
studieren	to study
einen Lehrgang besuchen	to go on a training course
ehrgeizig sein	to be ambitious
Erfahrung haben	to have experience
keine Erfahrung haben	to have no experience
arbeitslos sein	to be unemployed
erwerbslos sein	to be unemployed
Arbeit suchen	to look for work
auf Arbeitssuche sein	to be looking for work
sich für eine Stelle bewerben	to apply for a job
ablehnen	to reject
annehmen	to accept
einstellen	to take on
eine Stelle finden	to find a job
Erfolg haben	to be successful
seinen Lebensunterhalt verdienen	to earn a living
verdienen	to earn
bekommen	to get
bezahlen	to pay
Urlaub nehmen	to take a holiday
einen Tag frei nehmen	to take a day off
entlassen	to dismiss
kündigen	to resign
kündigen (+dat)	to dismiss
seine Stelle aufgeben	to leave
sich zur Ruhe setzen	to retire
streiken	to be on strike
in Streik treten	to go on strike, to strike

schwer	difficult
leicht	easy
interessant	interesting
aufregend	exciting
anregend	stimulating
reizvoll	challenging
langweilig	boring
eintönig	repetitive
gefährlich	dangerous
wichtig	important
nützlich	useful

Berufstätige

people at work

ein Angestellter, **eine Angestellte**	employee
ein(e) Ansager(in)	TV announcer
ein(e) Anstreicher(in)	painter and decorator
ein(e) Apotheker(in)	chemist
ein(e) Arbeiter(in)	(factory) worker
ein(e) Architekt(in)	architect
ein Arzt, eine Ärztin	doctor
ein(e) Astronaut(in)	astronaut
ein(e) Astronom(in)	astronomer
ein(e) Ausbilder(in)	instructor
eine Aushilfskraft	temp
ein Bäcker (*m*)	baker
ein Bankangestellter, **eine Bankangestellte**	bank clerk
ein Bauarbeiter (*m*)	builder, bricklayer
ein Bauer, eine Bäurin	farmer
ein Beamter, eine Beamtin	civil servant
ein Bergmann (*m*)	miner
ein(e) Berufsberater(in)	careers adviser
ein(e) Blumenhändler(in)	florist
ein(e) Buchhalter(in)	accountant
ein(e) Buchhändler(in)	bookseller
ein Büroangestellter, **eine Büroangestellte**	office worker

ein(e) Busfahrer(in)	bus driver
ein(e) Chirurg(in)	surgeon
ein(e) Diener(in)	servant
ein Dienstmädchen (*n*)	servant (*female*)
ein(e) Direktor(in)	manager, director
ein(e) Dolmetscher(in)	interpreter
ein(e) Dozent(in)	lecturer
ein(e) Drogist(in)	pharmacist
ein(e) Elektriker(in)	electrician
ein(e) Fahrer(in)	driver
ein Feuerwehrmann (*m*)	fireman
ein Fischer (*m*)	fisherman
ein(e) Fischhändler(in)	fishmonger
ein Fleischer (*m*)	butcher
ein(e) Fotograf(in)	photographer
ein Fotomodell (*n*)	model (*male and female*)
ein(e) Fremdenführer(in)	tourist guide
ein Friseur, eine Friseuse	hairdresser
ein(e) Gärtner(in)	gardener
ein Geistlicher (*m*)	priest
eine Geschäftsfrau	businesswoman
ein(e) Geschäftsführer(in)	manager, company director
ein(e) Geschäftsinhaber(in)	shopkeeper
ein Geschäftsmann (*m*)	businessman
ein(e) Grundschullehrer(in)	primary school teacher
ein Hausmeister (*m*)	caretaker
ein(e) Hilfsarbeiter(in)	labourer, unskilled worker
ein(e) Hochschullehrer(in)	university teacher
ein Ingenieur (*m*)	engineer
ein(e) Innenaustatter(in)	interior decorator
ein Installateur (*m*)	plumber
ein(e) Journalist(in)	journalist
ein Juwelier (*m*)	jeweller
ein Kaufmann, eine Kauffrau	shopkeeper; clerk
ein(e) Kellner(in)	waiter/waitress
ein(e) Kfz-Mechaniker(in)	garage mechanic
ein(e) Kindergärtner(in)	kindergarten teacher
ein Kindermädchen (*n*)	nanny
ein Klempner (*m*)	plumber

ein Koch, eine Köchin	cook
ein(e) Konditor(in)	confectioner, pastrycook
ein Krankenpfleger (m)	male nurse
eine Krankenschwester	(female) nurse
ein(e) Künstler(in)	artist
ein Lastwagenfahrer (m)	lorry driver
ein(e) Lebensmittelhändler(in)	grocer
ein(e) Lehrer(in)	teacher
ein Lieferant (m)	delivery man
ein(e) Maler(in)	painter
ein(e) Manager(in)	executive
ein Mannequin (n)	female model
ein Matrose (m)	sailor
ein(e) Mechaniker(in)	mechanic
ein Metzger (m)	butcher
ein(e) Möbelhändler(in)	furniture dealer
ein Möbelpacker (m)	removal man
ein(e) Moderator(in)	presenter (*on television, radio*)
ein(e) Modeschöpfer(in)	dressmaker, fashion designer
ein Mönch (m)	monk
ein Müllmann (m)	dustman
eine Nonne	nun
ein Ober (m)	waiter
ein Offizier (m)	(army) officer
ein(e) Pastor(in)	minister
ein(e) Physiker(in)	physicist
ein(e) Pilot(in)	pilot
eine Platzanweiserin	usherette
ein(e) Politiker(in)	politician
ein Polizist, eine Polizistin	policeman/woman
ein Postbote, eine Postbotin	postman/woman
ein Priester (m)	priest
ein(e) Psychiater(in)	psychiatrist
ein Psychologe, eine Psychologin	psychologist
eine Putzfrau	cleaner
eine Raumpflegerin	cleaner
ein Rechtsanwalt, eine Rechtsanwältin	lawyer

ein(e) Reporter(in)	reporter
ein(e) Richter(in)	judge
ein(e) Sänger(in)	singer
ein Sanitäter (*m*)	ambulance man
ein(e) Schäfer(in)	shepherd(ess)
ein(e) Schaffner(in)	(ticket) inspector, conductor
ein(e) Schauspieler(in)	actor/actress
ein(e) Schneider(in)	tailor
ein Schornsteinfeger (*m*)	chimneysweep
eine Schreibkraft	typist
ein Schreibwarenhändler (*m*)	stationer
ein(e) Schriftsteller(in)	writer
ein(e) Schuhmacher(in)	cobbler
ein(e) Schulleiter(in)	headteacher
ein Seemann (*m*)	sailor
eine Sekretärin	secretary (*female*)
ein Soldat (*m*)	soldier
ein(e) Sozialarbeiter(in)	social worker
eine Sprechstundenhilfe	receptionist, assistant
eine Stenotypistin	shorthand-typist
eine Stewardess	air hostess
ein(e) Student(in)	student
ein Studienrat, eine Studienrätin	secondary school teacher
ein(e) Taxifahrer(in)	taxi driver
ein(e) Techniker(in)	technician
ein(e) Telefonist(in)	switchboard operator
ein Tierarzt, eine Tierärztin	vet
ein(e) Übersetzer(in)	translator
ein(e) Uhrmacher(in)	watchmaker
ein(e) Verkäufer(in)	shop assistant, salesperson
ein(e) Vertreter(in)	sales representative
ein(e) Vorarbeiter(in)	foreman/woman
ein(e) Wissenschaftler(in)	scientist, scholar
ein Zahnarzt, eine Zahnärztin	dentist
ein(e) Zeichner(in)	graphic artist
ein(e) Zeitungshändler(in)	newsagent
ein Zimmermann (*m*)	carpenter

ein Zimmermädchen (*n*)	chambermaid
ein Zollbeamter, eine Zollbeamtin	customs officer

die Arbeitswelt

the world of work

ein(e) Arbeiter(in)	worker
ein Arbeitsloser, eine Arbeitslose	unemployed person
ein Arbeitssuchender, eine Arbeitssuchende	person seeking work
ein(e) Arbeitgeber(in)	employer
ein(e) Chef(in)	boss
die Geschäftsleitung	management
der Vorstand	board
ein(e) Arbeitnehmer(in)	employee
das Personal	staff, personnel
ein Kollege, eine Kollegin	colleague
ein Lehrling (*m*)	trainee, apprentice (*male and female*)
ein Auszubildender, eine Auszubildende	trainee, apprentice
ein Streikender, eine Streikende	striker
ein(e) Rentner(in)	retired person, pensioner
ein(e) Gewerkschafter(in)	trade unionist
ein Betriebsrat, eine Betriebsrätin	shop steward
die Zukunft	the future
eine Laufbahn	career
ein Beruf (*m*)	profession, occupation
die Branche	profession, line
eine Beschäftigung	job
Aussichten (*pl*)	prospects
Möglichkeiten (*pl*)	openings
eine Stelle	post
ein Lehrgang (*m*)	training course
die Lehrzeit	apprenticeship
die Ausbildung	training

die Weiterbildung	continuing education
ein Abschluß (*m*)	qualification, degree
eine Bescheinigung	certificate, diploma
eine Arbeit	job, employment
ein Job (*m*)	temporary job
eine Teilzeitarbeit	part-time job
eine Halbtagsbeschäftigung	part-time job
eine Ganztagsstelle	full-time job
die Kurzarbeit	short time
die Überstunden (*pl*)	overtime
die Berufsberatung	careers advice
der Bereich	sector
die Forschung	research
die Informatik	computer science
die Geschäftswelt	business
die Industrie	industry
ein Unternehmen (*n*)	company
ein Betrieb (*m*)	firm, factory
eine Firma	firm
ein Büro (*n*)	office
eine Fabrik	factory
eine Werkstatt	workshop
ein Geschäft (*n*)	shop
ein Labor (*n*)	laboratory
die Arbeit	work, job
die Mittagspause	lunch break
der Feierabend	end of work
der Urlaub	holidays
der Jahresurlaub	annual holiday
die Betriebsferien	company holidays
ein (Arbeits)vertrag (*m*)	contract of employment
eine Bewerbung	job application
ein Formular (*n*)	form
eine Anzeige	ad(vertisement)
Stellenangebote (*pl*)	situations vacant
das Vorstellungsgespräch	interview
das Gehalt	salary, wages
der (Arbeits)lohn	pay, wages
die gleitende Arbeitszeit	flexitime

die 40-Stunden-Woche	forty hour week
Steuern (*pl*)	taxes
eine Gehaltserhöhung	pay rise
eine Geschäftsreise	business trip
die Einstellung	appointment
die Entlassung	dismissal
die Rente	pension
die Gewerkschaft	trade union
der Streik	strike
der Bummelstreik	go-slow
ein wilder Streik	wildcat strike
der Dienst nach Vorschrift	work-to-rule

was ist er/sie von Beruf?
what does he/she do for a living?

er ist Arzt
he's a doctor

was möchtest du einmal werden?
what do you want to be?

was sind Ihre Zukunftspläne?
what are your plans for the future?

ich wäre gern ein Künstler
I'd like to be an artist

ich will Medizin studieren
I intend to study medicine

er ist krank geschrieben
he is on sick-leave

am wichtigsten ist mit die Bezahlung/die Freizeit
what matters most for me is the pay/free time

Feierabend machen
to finish work

ich verbringe den Feierabend mit Freunden
after work I get together with my friends

am meisten interessiert mich das Theater
what I'm most interested in is the theatre

11. CHARAKTER UND BENEHMEN
CHARACTER AND BEHAVIOUR

sich benehmen	to behave
sich verhalten	to behave
sich beherrschen	to control oneself
gehorchen	to obey
erlauben	to allow
lassen	to let
verhindern	to prevent
verbieten	to forbid
billigen	to approve of
mißbilligen	to disapprove of
ausschimpfen	to scold
ausgeschimpft werden	to be told off
sich aufregen	to get angry
sich entschuldigen	to apologize
vergeben	to forgive
bestrafen	to punish
belohnen	to reward
wagen	to dare
die Arroganz	arrogance
das Benehmen	behaviour
der Charakter	character
der Charme	charm
die Ehrlichkeit	honesty
die Eifersucht	jealousy
die Einsicht	insight, understanding
die Eitelkeit	vanity
eine Entschuldigung	excuse, apology
die Erlaubnis	permission
die Faulheit	laziness
die Frechheit	insolence
die Freude	joy, delight
die Fröhlichkeit	cheerfulness
die Geduld	patience
die Gehässigkeit	spite

der Gehorsam	obedience
die Geschicklichkeit	skilfulness
die Grausamkeit	cruelty
die Grobheit	coarseness
die Güte	goodness, kindness
die Höflichkeit	politeness
der Instinkt	instinct
die Intelligenz	intelligence
die Intoleranz	intolerance
die Laune	mood
die Liebenswürdigkeit	kindness
die Menschlichkeit	humanity
der Neid	envy
die Prahlerei	boastfulness
die Rücksichtslosigkeit	heedlessness
die Schlauheit	craftiness
die Schüchternheit	shyness, timidity
die Stimmung	mood
der Stolz	pride
die Strafe	punishment
die Trauer	sadness
die Ungeduld	impatience
die Ungezogenheit	nastiness, naughtiness
die Unhöflichkeit	rudeness
das Verhalten	behaviour
die Verlegenheit	embarrassment
die Verrücktheit	folly, madness
die Vorsicht	caution
aktiv	active
amüsant	amusing
angeberisch	pretentious
angenehm	nice, pleasant
anständig	decent
arm	poor
arrogant	arrogant
bescheiden	modest
besitzergreifend	possessive
blöd	silly, stupid
böse	angry

boshaft	mischievous
charmant	charming
doof	stupid, daft
dumm	stupid
ehrbar	respectable
ehrlich	honest
eifersüchtig	jealous
einsichtig	understanding
eitel	vain
ernst	serious
erstaunlich	surprising
faul	lazy
fleißig	industrious
frech	cheeky
freundlich	friendly
froh	glad
fröhlich	joyful, cheerful
geduldig	patient
gehorsam	obedient
geistreich	witty
geschickt	skilful
gesprächig	talkative
gleichgültig	indifferent
glücklich	happy
grausam	cruel
grob	rude, coarse
gut	good
gutgelaunt	cheerful
gütig	kind
hartnäckig	obstinate
herrlich	terrific
hinterhältig	devious, shifty
höflich	polite
impulsiv	impulsive
instinktiv	instinctive
intelligent	intelligent
intolerant	intolerant
komisch	funny
langweilig	boring
lästig	annoying

liebevoll	affectionate
lustig	funny
mutig	courageous
naiv	naive
natürlich	natural
neidisch	envious
nett	kind, nice
neugierig	curious
optimistisch	optimistic
pessimistisch	pessimistic
prahlerisch	boastful
raffiniert	shrewd
respektvoll	respectful
ruhig	quiet, calm
sanftmütig	gentle
scharfsinnig	astute
schlau	wily
schlecht	bad
schlechtgelaunt	in a bad mood
schüchtern	shy, timid
seltsam	strange
sensibel	sensitive
stolz	proud
störrisch	stubborn
sympathisch	nice, pleasant
tolerant	tolerant
toll	terrific
tolpatschig	clumsy, cack-handed
traurig	sad
unangenehm	nasty
ungeduldig	impatient
unfreundlich	unfriendly
ungehorsam	disobedient
ungeschickt	clumsy
ungesellig	unsociable
ungezogen	mischievous, naughty
unglücklich	unhappy
unhöflich	rude
unordentlich	untidy
unverschämt	insolent

unzugänglich	unapproachable
verlegen	embarrassed
vernünftig	sensible, reasonable
verrückt	mad
verschwiegen	discreet
vorsichtig	cautious, careful
zerfahren	scatterbrained
zerstreut	absent-minded
zufrieden	pleased

ich finde sie sehr nett
I think she's very nice

er hat (sehr) gute/schlechte Laune
he's in a (very) good/bad mood

er hat eine sehr zurückhaltende Art
he is very shy and retiring

er ist gutmütig/übellaunig
he is good/ill-natured

sie ist von Natur aus sehr schüchtern
she is very shy by nature

sie war so nett, mir ihr Auto zu leihen
she was good enough to lend me her car

er ist ein Angeber
he's a show-off

es tut mir (sehr) leid
I'm (really) sorry

ich bitte vielmals um Entschuldigung
I do apologize

er entschuldigte sich beim Lehrer für seine Frechheiten
he apologized to the teacher for being cheeky

12. GEFÜHLE
EMOTIONS

Wut anger

wütend werden	to become angry
die Fassung verlieren	to lose one's temper
böse sein	to be angry
wütend sein	to be fuming
mürrisch sein	to be sullen/morose
sich ärgern	to be/get angry
verärgert sein	to be angry/annoyed
sich entrüsten	to be/get indignant
sich aufregen	to get excited/worked up
schreien	to shout
brüllen	to yell
schlagen	to hit
ohrfeigen	to slap (on the face)

die Wut	anger
die Entrüstung	indignation
der Ärger	anger
die Spannung	tension
der Schrei	cry, shout
der Schlag	blow
die Ohrfeige	slap (on the face)

Trauer sadness

weinen	to weep, to cry
in Tränen ausbrechen	to burst into tears
schluchzen	to sob
seufzen	to sigh

Sorge bereiten (+dat)	to distress
schockieren	to shock
bestürzen	to dismay

enttäuschen	to disappoint
beunruhigen	to disconcert
deprimieren	to depress
berühren	to move, to affect, to touch
bekümmern	to trouble
Mitleid haben	to take pity
trösten	to comfort, to console
die Sorge	grief, sorrow
die Trauer	sadness
die Enttäuschung	disappointment
die Depression	depression
das Heimweh	homesickness
die Melancholie	melancholy
das Leiden	suffering
eine Träne	tear
ein Schluchzen (n)	sob
ein Seufzer (m)	sigh
das Versagen	failure
das Pech	bad luck
das Unglück	misfortune, bad luck
traurig	sad
mitgenommen	shattered
enttäuscht	disappointed
deprimiert	depressed
ernüchtert	disenchanted
frustriert	frustrated
bekümmert	distressed, sorry
berührt	moved, touched
melancholisch	gloomy
mißmutig	morose
unglücklich	unhappy

Angst und Sorge — fear and worry

Angst haben (vor)	to be frightened (of)
fürchten	to fear
erschrecken	to frighten

Angst machen	to frighten
sich sorgen wegen	to worry about
zittern	to tremble
die Angst	fear
die Furcht	fear
der Schrecken	fright
der Schauer	shiver
der Schock	shock
das Herzklopfen	palpitations
die Bestürzung	consternation
der Ärger	trouble
die Ängste (*pl*)	anxieties
ein Problem (*n*)	problem
eine Sorge	worry
furchtsam	fearful
ängstlich	afraid
erschreckt	frightened
besorgt	worried, anxious
nervös	nervous

Glück und Freude   joy and happiness

sich amüsieren	to enjoy oneself
erfreut sein über (*+acc*)	to be delighted about
lachen (**über** *+acc*)	to laugh (at)
in Gelächter ausbrechen	to burst out laughing
kichern	to have the giggles
lächeln	to smile
das Glück	happiness
die Freude	joy
die Zufriedenheit	satisfaction
das Lachen	laugh
ein Lachanfall (*m*)	fit of laughter
eine Lachsalve	burst of laughter
das Gelächter	laughter
ein Lächeln (*n*)	smile
die Liebe	love

das Glück	luck
der Erfolg	success
die Überraschung	surprise
zufrieden	pleased
erfreut	happy
hocherfreut	overjoyed
strahlend	radiant
verliebt	in love

er hat sie erschreckt
he frightened them/her

er hat Angst vor Hunden
he's frightened of dogs

er war starr vor Schrecken
he was petrified

es tut mir sehr leid, das zu hören
I'm very sorry to learn this news

sein Bruder fehlt ihm
he misses his brother

ich habe Heimweh
I'm homesick

ich habe keine Lust dazu
I don't feel like it

sein Erfolg machte ihn sehr froh
his success made him very happy

sie hat Glück
she is lucky

er ist in Hilde verliebt
he's in love with Hilde

13. DIE SINNE
THE SENSES

Sicht	sight
sehen	to see
betrachten	to look at, to watch
beobachten	to observe, to watch
untersuchen	to examine, to study closely
erblicken	to catch sight of
blicken (auf +*acc*)	to look at
einen Blick werfen auf (+*acc*)	to glance at
starren auf (+*acc*)	to stare at
gucken auf (+*acc*)	to peek at
das Licht anmachen	to switch on the light
das Licht ausmachen	to switch off the light
blenden	to dazzle, to blind
erscheinen	to appear
verschwinden	to disappear
wieder auftauchen	to reappear
fernsehen	to watch TV
unter dem Mikroskop betrachten	to observe under the microscope
der Blick	view
der Gesichtssinn	sight (*sense*)
der Anblick	sight (*seen*)
das Sehvermögen	vision
die Farbe	colour
das Licht	light
die Helligkeit	brightness
die Dunkelheit	darkness
das Auge	eye
eine Brille	glasses

eine Sonnenbrille	sun glasses
Kontaktlinsen (*pl*)	contact lenses
eine Lupe	magnifying glass
ein Vergrößerungsglas (*n*)	magnifying glass
ein Fernglas (*n*)	binoculars
ein Mikroskop (*n*)	microscope
ein Teleskop (*n*)	telescope
die Blindenschrift	Braille
hell	bright, light
blendend	dazzling
dunkel	dark
finster	dark

Gehör   hearing

hören	to hear
zuhören (+*dat*)	to listen to
flüstern	to whisper
singen	to sing
summen	to hum
brummen	to drone
pfeifen	to whistle
rascheln	to rustle
knistern	to crackle
knarren	to creak
läuten	to ring
donnern	to thunder
surren	to hum (*engine*)
rauschen	to rush (*water*)
still sein	to be silent
die Ohren spitzen	to prick up one's ears
die Tür zuknallen	to slam the door
die Schallmauer durchbrechen	to break the sound barrier
das Gehör	hearing
das Geräusch	noise, sound
der Ton	sound

der Lärm	racket
das Echo	echo
das Flüstern	whisper
das Lied	song
das Summen	buzzing
das Rascheln	rustling
das Knistern	crackling
die Explosion	explosion
das Knarren	creaking
das Läuten	ringing
der Donner	thunder
das Ohr	ear
der Lautsprecher	loudspeaker
die Lautsprecheranlage	public address system
eine Gegensprechanlage	intercom
Kopfhörer (*pl*)	earphones, headset
der Walkman (*R*)	personal stereo
das Radio	radio
die Sirene	siren
das Morsealphabet	Morse code
das Ohropax (*R*)	earplugs
ein Hörgerät (*n*)	hearing-aid
laut	noisy, loud
leise	quiet
still	silent
melodisch	melodious
schwach	faint
ohrenbetäubend	deafening
taub	deaf
schwerhörig	hard of hearing

Tastsinn   touch

berühren	to touch
streicheln	to stroke
fühlen	to feel
kitzeln	to tickle
reiben	to rub
stoßen	to knock

schlagen	to hit
kratzen	to scratch
die Berührung	touch
die Kälte	cold
die Wärme	warm
das Streicheln	stroke
der Stoß	knock
der Schlag	blow
der Händedruck	handshake
Fingerspitzen (*pl*)	fingertips
glatt	smooth
rauh	rough
weich	soft
hart	hard
warm	warm
heiß	hot
kalt	cold

Geschmack   taste

probieren	to taste
trinken	to drink
essen	to eat
lecken	to lick
schlürfen	to sip
verschlingen	to gobble up
kosten	to savour
schlucken	to swallow
kauen	to chew
salzen	to salt
pfeffern	to put pepper on
zuckern	to sugar
süßen	to sweeten
würzen	to spice
der Geschmack	taste
der Mund	mouth
die Zunge	tongue

der Speichel	saliva
Geschmacksknospen (*pl*)	taste buds
der Appetit	appetite
der Hunger	hunger
appetitlich	appetizing
appetitanregend	appetizing
köstlich	delicious
scheußlich	horrible
süß	sweet
zuckrig	sugary
salzig	salted, salty
herb	tart
sauer	sour
bitter	bitter
ranzig	rancid
scharf	spicy, hot
streng	pungent
fade	tasteless
lecker	delicious

Geruch   smell

riechen (nach)	to smell (of)
wittern	to scent, to detect
schnüffeln	to sniff
stinken	to stink
parfümieren	to perfume
gut/schlecht riechen	to smell nice/nasty
der Geruchssinn	sense of smell
der Geruch	smell
der Duft	scent
das Parfüm	perfume
das Aroma	aroma, fragrance
der Gestank	stench, stink
der Rauch	smoke
die Nase	nose
Nasenlöcher (*pl*)	nostrils

parfümiert	fragrant, scented
stinkend	stinking
verräuchert	smoky (*room*)
geruchlos	odourless

im Keller ist es dunkel
it's dark in the cellar

ich habe das Kind singen hören
I heard the child singing

ich höre dich nicht
I can't hear you

es fühlt sich weich an
it feels soft

dabei läuft mir das Wasser im Mund zusammen
it makes my mouth water

dieser Kaffee schmeckt nach Seife
this coffee tastes of soap

es riecht gut/schlecht
it smells good/bad

in diesem Zimmer riecht es nach Rauch
this room smells of smoke

hier ist es stickig
it's stuffy in here

See also Sections **4 BODY, 6 HEALTH, 16 FOOD** *and* **62 COLOURS**.

14. VORLIEBEN UND ABNEIGUNGEN
LIKES AND DISLIKES

mögen	to like
gern haben	to like
lieben	to love
eine Vorliebe für etwas haben	to have a liking for something
schwärmen für	to adore, to be mad about
anbeten	to idolize
nicht mögen	to dislike
verabscheuen	to detest
hassen	to hate
verachten	to despise
ablehnen	to reject
vorziehen	to prefer
lieber mögen	to prefer
wählen	to choose
zögern	to hesitate
beschließen	to decide
vergleichen	to compare
brauchen	to need
benötigen	to need
wollen	to want, to wish for
(sich) wünschen	to wish for
hoffen	to hope
die Liebe	love
der Geschmack	taste
die Vorliebe	liking, preference
das Interesse	interest
die Abneigung	strong dislike
der Haß	hate
die Verachtung	scorn

die Wahl	choice
der Vergleich	comparison
das Gegenteil	contrary, opposite
der Kontrast	contrast
der Unterschied	difference
die Ähnlichkeit	similarity
das Bedürfnis	need
der Wunsch	wish, desire
Lieblings-	favourite
vergleichbar (mit)	comparable (to)
verschieden (von)	different (from)
anders (als)	different (from)
identisch (mit)	identical (to)
dasselbe (wie)	the same (as)
das gleiche (wie)	the same (as)
ähnlich	similar
wie	like
im Vergleich zu	in comparison with
in bezug auf (+*acc*)	in relation to
mehr	more
weniger	less
viel	a lot
eine Menge	enormously, a great deal
viel mehr/weniger	a lot more/less
sehr viel mehr/weniger	quite a lot more/less
besser	better

mir/ihnen gefällt dieses Buch
I/they like this book

rot ist meine Lieblingsfarbe
red is my favourite colour

ich mag lieber Tee als Kaffee
I prefer tea to coffee

ich kann ... nicht ausstehen
I can't stand ...

das gefällt mir gar nicht
I don't like that at all

ich bleibe lieber zu Hause
I'd rather stay at home

es freut mich, Sie zu sehen
I'm pleased to see you

ich möchte gern ausgehen
I'd like to go out

hoffentlich kommt er bald
I hope he comes soon

TAGESABLAUF UND SCHLAF
DAILY ROUTINE AND SLEEP

aufwachen	to wake up
erwachen	to wake up
aufstehen	to get up
sich strecken	to stretch
gähnen	to yawn
ausgeschlafen sein	to have had a good sleep
einen Kater haben	to have a hangover
sich ausschlafen	to have a long lie
verschlafen	to oversleep
die Vorhänge öffnen	to open the curtains
sich waschen	to wash
sich (*dat*) das Gesicht waschen	to wash one's face
sich (*dat*) die Hände waschen	to wash one's hands
sich (*dat*) die Zähne putzen	to brush one's teeth
sich (*dat*) die Haare waschen	to wash one's hair
duschen	to have a shower
baden	to have a bath
ein Bad (*n*) nehmen	to have a bath
sich einseifen	to soap oneself down
sich abtrocknen	to dry oneself
sich (*dat*) die Hände abtrocknen	to dry one's hands
sich rasieren	to shave
auf die Toilette gehen	to go to the toilet
sich anziehen	to get dressed
sich (*dat*) die Haare kämmen	to comb one's hair
sich (*dat*) die Haare bürsten	to brush one's hair
sich schminken	to put on make-up
die Brille aufsetzen	to put one's glasses on
sich im Spiegel betrachten	to look at oneself in the mirror

das Bett machen	to make the bed
das Radio/Fernsehen einschalten	to switch the radio/television on
das Radio/Fernsehen ausschalten	to switch the radio/television off
frühstücken	to have breakfast
die Katze/den Hund füttern	to feed the cat/dog
die Blumen gießen	to water the plants
sich fertigmachen	to get ready
das Haus verlassen	to leave the house
zur Schule gehen	to go to school
ins Büro gehen	to go to the office
zur Arbeit gehen	to go to work
mit dem Bus/der Straßenbahn fahren	to take the bus/tram
nach Hause gehen/kommen	to go/come home
aus der Schule (zurück)kommen	to come back from school
von der Arbeit (zurück)kommen	to come back from work
die Hausaufgaben machen	to do one's homework
sich ausruhen	to have a rest
ein Nickerchen (n) machen	to have a nap
fernsehen	to watch television
lesen	to read
spielen	to play
zu Mittag essen	to have lunch
zu Abend essen	to have dinner
die Tür abschließen	to lock the door
sich ausziehen	to undress
die Vorhänge zuziehen	to draw the curtains
zu Bett gehen	to go to bed
sich zudecken	to tuck oneself up
den Wecker stellen	to set the alarm clock
das Licht ausmachen	to switch the light off
einschlafen	to fall asleep
schlafen	to sleep
nicht einschlafen können	not to be able to get to sleep

an Schlaflosigkeit leiden	to suffer from insomnia
eine schlaflose Nacht verbringen	to have a sleepless night
schlafwandeln	to sleepwalk
eine Schlaftablette nehmen	to take a sleeping pill

Waschen   washing

die Seife	soap
das Handtuch	towel
das Bade(hand)tuch	bath towel
das Händehandtuch	hand towel
der Waschlappen	flannel
ein Schwamm (*m*)	sponge
eine Bürste	brush
ein Kamm (*m*)	comb
eine Zahnbürste	toothbrush
die Zahnpasta	toothpaste
das Shampoo	shampoo
das Schaumbad	bubble bath
das Badesalz	bath salts
das Deo	deodorant
das Toilettenpapier	toilet paper
der Haartrockner	hair dryer
der Fön (*R*)	hair dryer
die Waage	scales

Bett   bed

ein Kopfkissen (*n*)	pillow
eine Nackenrolle	bolster
die Bettwäsche	bed linen
ein (Bett)laken (*n*)	sheet
eine Decke	blanket
eine Steppdecke	continental quilt
ein Federbett (*n*)	duvet
die Matratze	mattress
die Tagesdecke	bedspread

eine Heizdecke	electric blanket
eine Wärmflasche	hot-water bottle
gewöhnlich	usually
morgens	in the morning
mittags	at midday, at lunchtime
abends	in the evening
nachts	at night
dann	then

ich stelle den Wecker auf sieben Uhr
I set my alarm clock for seven

ich bin kein Nachtschwärmer; ich gehe früh zu Bett
I'm not a night owl; I go to bed early

ich habe geschlafen wie ein Bär
I slept like a log

er kommt immer zu spät zur Schule
he's always late for school

ich bin nicht ausgeschlafen
I didn't get enough sleep/I'm not awake yet

See also Sections **16 FOOD, 17 HOUSEWORK, 23 MY ROOM** *and* **54 ADVENTURES AND DREAMS**.

16. ESSEN
FOOD

essen	to eat
trinken	to drink
probieren	to taste, to try

Mahlzeiten — meals

das Frühstück	breakfast
das Mittagessen	lunch
das Abendessen	dinner
das Abendbrot	dinner
das Essen	food
ein Imbiß (*m*)	snack
die Zwischenmahlzeit	snack
das Picknick	picnic
ein Menü (*n*)	set menu
ein Kinderteller (*m*)	children's portion
eine Portion	helping

Gänge — courses

die Vorspeise	starter, hors d'oeuvre
die Tagessuppe	soup of the day
das Hauptgericht	main course
das Tagesgericht	today's special (*in a restaurant*)
der Nachtisch	sweet
die Nachspeise	dessert
der Käse	cheese

Getränke — drinks

das Wasser	water

das Mineralwasser	mineral water
die Milch	milk
der Tee	tea
der Pfefferminztee	mint tea
der Kamillentee	camomile tea
der Kaffee	coffee
ein Kännchen (n) Kaffee	pot of coffee
ein Kakao (m)	hot chocolate
ein Fruchtsaft (m)	fruit juice
ein Apfelsaft (m)	apple juice
ein Orangensaft (m)	orange juice
eine Cola	coke (R)
eine Limonade	lemonade
ein Bier (n)	beer
ein Pils (n)	pils
ein Malzbier (n)	malt beer
ein Alsterwasser (n)	shandy
ein Cidre (m)	cider
der Wein	wine
der Rotwein	red wine
der Weißwein	white wine
der Rosé	rosé wine
der Sekt	champagne
der Champagner	champagne
ein Aperitif (m)	aperitif
ein Likör (m)	liqueur
ein Schnaps (m)	schnapps
ein Kognak (m)	cognac
ein Weinbrand (m)	brandy

Gewürze

seasonings and herbs

das Salz	salt
der Pfeffer	pepper
der Zucker	sugar
der Senf	mustard
der Essig	vinegar
das Öl	oil
der Knoblauch	garlic
die Zwiebel	onion

Gewürze (*pl*)	spices
Kräuter (*pl*)	herbs
die Petersilie	parsley
ein Lorbeerblatt (*n*)	bay leaf
der Muskat	nutmeg
eine Gewürznelke	clove
der Ingwer	ginger
die Soße	sauce
die Mayonnaise	mayonnaise

Frühstück   breakfast

das Brot	bread
das Weißbrot	white bread
das Graubrot	brown bread
ein Brötchen (*n*)	roll
der Zwieback	rusk
das Knäckebrot	crispbread
ein Butterbrot (*n*)	bread and butter
ein Honigbrot (*n*)	bread and honey
ein Käsebrot (*n*)	bread and cheese
ein belegtes Brot	sandwich
ein Butterbrot (*n*)	piece of bread and butter
der Toast	toast
die Butter	butter
die Margarine	margarine
die Marmelade	jam
die Konfitüre	jam
die Orangenmarmelade	marmalade
der Honig	honey
die Corn-flakes (*R*)	cornflakes

Obst   fruit

eine Frucht	piece of fruit
ein Apfel (*m*)	apple
eine Birne	pear
eine Aprikose	apricot
ein Pfirsich (*m*)	peach

eine Pflaume	plum
eine Melone	melon
eine Ananas	pineapple
eine Banane	banana
eine Orange	orange
eine Apfelsine	orange
eine Pampelmuse	grapefruit
eine Mandarine	tangerine
eine Zitrone	lemon
eine Erdbeere	strawberry
eine Himbeere	raspberry
eine Brombeere	blackberry
eine rote Johannisbeere	redcurrant
eine schwarze Johannisbeere	blackcurrant
eine Kirsche	cherry
(Wein)trauben (*pl*)	grapes

Gemüse   vegetables

ein Gemüse (*n*)	vegetable
Erbsen (*pl*)	peas
grüne Bohnen (*pl*)	green beans
der Lauch	leeks
der Porree	leeks
eine Kartoffel	potato
die Salzkartoffeln (*pl*)	boiled potatoes
die Pommes frites (*pl*)	chips
die Chips (*pl*)	crisps
der Kartoffelsalat	potato salad
das Kartoffelpüree	mashed potatoes
der Kartoffelbrei	mashed potatoes
Pellkartoffeln (*pl*)	jacket potatoes
Knödel (*pl*)	dumplings
eine Möhre	carrot
der Kohl	cabbage
der Weißkohl	white cabbage
das Sauerkraut	sauerkraut
der Rotkohl	red cabbage
der Grünkohl	kale

der Blumenkohl	cauliflower
der Rosenkohl	Brussels sprouts
der Kopfsalat	lettuce
der Spinat	spinach
Pilze (*pl*)	mushrooms
ein Champignon (*m*)	button mushroom
eine Artischocke	artichoke
der Spargel	asparagus
eine (grüne/rote) Paprikaschote	(green/red) pepper
eine Aubergine	aubergine
die Brokkoli (*pl*)	broccoli
die Zucchini (*pl*)	courgettes
eine Zwiebel	onion
der Mais	corn
der Rettich	radish
die Radieschen (*pl*)	radishes
eine Tomate	tomato
eine Gurke	cucumber
die Beilage	side dish
ein gemischter Salat	mixed salad
der Reis	rice
Nudeln (*pl*)	pasta, noodles
eine kalte Platte	salad

Fleisch   meat

das Schweinefleisch	pork
das Kalbfleisch	veal
das Rindfleisch	beef
das Lammfleisch	lamb
das Hammelfleisch	mutton
das Rehfleisch	venison
ein Hähnchen (*n*)	chicken
ein Brathähnchen (*n*)	roast chicken
ein Truthahn (*m*)	turkey
eine Ente	duck
eine Gans	goose
das Geflügel	poultry

ein Hase (*m*)	hare
das Wild	game
ein Steak (*n*)	steak
ein Beefsteak (*n*)	steak
ein Kotelett (*n*)	chop
ein Schnitzel (*n*)	escalope
ein Wiener Schnitzel (*n*)	Wiener schnitzel
ein Braten (*m*)	joint
ein Schweinebraten (*m*)	roast pork
das Roastbeef	roast beef
das Ragout	stew
der Gulasch	goulash
das Hackfleisch	mince
die Frikadelle	meatball
ein deutsches Beefsteak	hamburger
der Hamburger	hamburger
Nieren (*pl*)	kidneys
die Leber	liver
der Schinken	ham
die Leberpastete	liver pâté
die Wurst	sausage
der Aufschnitt	slices of cold meat
die Leberwurst	liver sausage
die Blutwurst	black pudding
eine Bratwurst	sausage (*fried or grilled*)
eine Bockwurst	sausage (*boiled*)
eine Currywurst	curried sausage
ein Würstchen (*n*)	frankfurter
der Speck	bacon

Fisch   fish

der Rotbarsch	rosefish
der Kabeljau	cod
Ölsardinen (*pl*)	sardines
die Scholle	sole
der Thunfisch	tuna fish
die Forelle	trout
der Lachs	salmon

der Räucherlachs	smoked salmon
Fischstäbchen (*n*)	fish fingers
die Meeresfrüchte (*pl*)	seafood
der Hummer	lobster
Austern (*pl*)	oysters
Krabben (*pl*)	prawns
Muscheln (*pl*)	mussels

Eier — eggs

ein Ei (*n*)	egg
ein gekochtes Ei	boiled egg
ein Spiegelei (*n*)	fried egg
Eier mit Speck	ham and eggs
Rührei (*n*)	scrambled eggs
verlorene Eier	poached eggs
ein Omelett (*n*)	omelette

Nudeln — pasta

die Spaghetti (*pl*)	spaghetti
die Makkaroni (*pl*)	macaroni
die Spätzle (*pl*)	type of home-made pasta

warme Gerichte — hot dishes

die Suppe	soup
ein Auflauf (*m*)	soufflé
ein Pfannkuchen (*m*)	pancake
das Eisbein	knuckle of pork
der Sauerbraten	marinated potroast
gekocht	cooked, boiled
durchgebraten	well done (*meat*)
englisch	rare (*meat*)
paniert	breaded
am Spieß	spit-roast
gefüllt	stuffed
gebraten	fried, roast

gebacken	roast, baked
überbacken	baked in the oven with cheese

Nachtisch — desserts

eine Apfeltorte	apple tart
die Sahne	cream
die Schlagsahne	whipped cream
ein Eis (*n*)	ice-cream
ein Vanilleeis (*n*)	vanilla ice-cream
eine Käseplatte	selection of cheeses
ein Pudding (*m*)	blancmange, jelly *etc*
der Schokoladenpudding	chocolate dessert
der Joghurt	yoghurt
die Vanillesoße	custard

Süßigkeiten — sweet things

die Schokolade	chocolate
eine Tafel Schokolade	chocolate bar
Pralinen (*pl*)	chocolates
Plätzchen (*pl*)	biscuits
Kekse (*pl*)	biscuits
ein Kuchen (*m*)	cake
eine Torte	gateau, tart
eine Eissplittertorte	ice-chip gateau
eine Schwarzwälder Kirschtorte	Black Forest gateau
ein Käsekuchen (*m*)	cheesecake
ein Eis (*n*) **am Stiel**	ice lolly
Bonbons (*pl*)	sweets
Pfefferminzbonbons	mints
der Kaugummi	chewing gum

Geschmacksrichtungen tastes

der Geschmack	taste

das Aroma	aroma
süß	sweet
salzig	salty
bitter	bitter
sauer	sour
würzig	spicy
pikant	savoury
scharf	hot
fade	tasteless

Tabak   tobacco

eine Zigarette	cigarette
eine Zigarre	cigar
ein Zigarillo (*n*)	cigarillo
eine Pfeife	pipe
ein Streichholz (*n*)	match
ein Feuerzeug (*n*)	cigarette lighter
eine Schachtel Zigaretten	packet of cigarettes
ein Päckchen (*n*) **Tabak**	packet of tobacco
eine Filterzigarette	filter-tipped cigarette
der Pfeifentabak	pipe tobacco
die Streichholzschachtel	box of matches
die Asche	ash
ein Aschenbecher (*m*)	ashtray
der Rauch	smoke
rauchen	to smoke
anzünden	to light
ausdrücken	to stub out

> **haben Sie Feuer?**
> have you got a light?

See also Sections **5 HOW ARE YOU FEELING?, 17 HOUSEWORK, 60 QUANTITIES** *and* **61 DESCRIBING THINGS**.

17. HAUSHALT
HOUSEWORK

die Hausarbeit machen	to do the housework
kochen	to cook
das Essen zubereiten	to prepare a meal
abwaschen	to do the washing-up
spülen	to do the washing-up
abtrocknen	to do the drying-up
(Wäsche) waschen	to do the washing
saubermachen	to clean
kehren	to sweep
wegwerfen	to throw away
Staub putzen	to dust
staubsaugen	to vacuum
aufräumen	to tidy up
das Bett machen	to make the bed
vorbereiten	to prepare
schneiden	to cut
in Scheiben schneiden	to slice
reiben	to grate
schälen	to peel
kochen	to cook, to boil
braten	to fry, to roast
grillen	to grill
rösten	to toast
den Tisch decken	to set the table
den Tisch abräumen	to clear the table
bügeln	to iron
nähen	to sew
stopfen	to darn
reparieren	to mend
flicken	to patch
sich kümmern um (+*dat*)	to look after
helfen	to help
zur Hand gehen (+*dat*)	to give a hand

im Haus Beschäftigte

people who work in the house

die Hausfrau	housewife
die Putzfrau	cleaner
eine Haushaltshilfe	home help
ein Dienstmädchen (*n*)	maid
ein Au-pair-Mädchen (*n*)	au pair
ein(e) Babysitter(in)	baby sitter

Haushaltsgeräte

household appliances

ein Staubsauger (*m*)	vacuum-cleaner
eine Waschmaschine	washing machine
eine Wäscheschleuder	spin-dryer
ein Trockenautomat (*m*)	tumbledryer
ein Bügeleisen (*n*)	iron
eine Nähmaschine	sewing machine
eine Küchenmaschine	blender
ein Mixer (*m*)	mixer, liquidizer
eine Kaffeemühle	coffee grinder
ein Mikrowellenherd (*m*)	microwave oven
ein Kühlschrank (*m*)	fridge
eine Tiefkühltruhe	freezer
eine (Geschirr)spülmaschine	dish-washer
ein Herd (*m*)	cooker
ein Elektroherd (*m*)	electric cooker
ein Gasherd (*m*)	gas cooker
der Backofen	oven
das Gas	gas
der Strom	electricity, power
ein Toaster (*m*)	toaster
ein Wasserkessel (*m*)	kettle

Zubehör

utensils

ein Bügelbrett (*n*)	ironing board
ein Besen (*m*)	broom
ein Kehrblech (*n*) und ein Handfeger (*m*)	brush and dustpan
ein Abfalleimer (*m*)	(rubbish) bin
eine Bürste	brush
ein Lappen (*m*)	rag
ein Putzlappen (*m*)	floorcloth
ein Staubtuch (*n*)	cloth, duster
ein Spültuch (*n*)	dish cloth
ein Geschirrtuch (*n*)	dish towel
ein Waschbecken (*n*)	washhand basin
die Spüle	sink
eine Spülschüssel	basin
ein Topfhandschuh (*m*)	oven glove
ein Wäscheständer (*m*)	clothes horse
das (Geschirr)spülmittel	washing-up liquid
das Waschpulver	washing powder
ein Kochtopf (*m*)	saucepan
eine (Brat)pfanne	frying pan
eine Kasserolle	casserole dish
ein Dampfkochtopf (*m*)	pressure cooker
ein Schnellkochtopf (*m*)	pressure cooker
eine Friteuse	chip pan
eine Teigrolle	rolling pin
ein Brett (*n*)	board
ein Dosenöffner (*m*)	tin opener
ein Flaschenöffner (*m*)	bottle opener
ein Korkenzieher (*m*)	corkscrew
eine Knoblauchpresse	garlic press
ein Schneebesen (*m*)	whisk
ein Tablett (*n*)	tray

Besteck

cutlery

das Besteck	cutlery

ein Löffel (*m*)	spoon
ein Kaffeelöffel (*m*)	teaspoon
ein Eßlöffel (*m*)	soupspoon, tablespoon
eine Gabel	fork
eine Kuchengabel	pastry fork
ein Messer (*n*)	knife
ein Küchenmesser (*n*)	kitchen knife
ein Brotmesser (*n*)	bread knife
ein Schälmesser (*n*)	peeler

Geschirr   dishes

das Geschirr	dishes
ein Set (*n*)	place mat
ein Teller (*m*)	plate
eine Untertasse	saucer
eine Tasse	cup
ein Glas (*n*)	glass
ein Weinglas (*n*)	wine glass
ein Suppenteller (*m*)	soup plate
eine Suppenschüssel	soup tureen
eine Schale	dish, bowl (*shallow*)
eine Schüssel	dish, bowl (*large*)
ein Salzstreuer (*m*)	salt cellar
ein Pfefferstreuer (*m*)	pepper pot
eine Pfeffermühle	pepper-mill
eine Zuckerdose	sugar bowl
eine Teekanne	teapot
eine Kaffeekanne	coffeepot
ein Milchkännchen (*n*)	milk jug

mein Vater spült das Geschirr
my father does the dishes

meine Eltern teilen sich die Hausarbeit
my parents share the housework

See also Sections **16 FOOD** *and* **24 THE HOUSE**.

18. EINKAUFEN
SHOPPING

kaufen	to buy
kosten	to cost
ausgeben	to spend
umtauschen	to exchange
(be)zahlen	to pay
Wechselgeld herausgeben	to give change
verkaufen	to sell
anbieten	to offer
einkaufen gehen	to go shopping
einkaufen	to do the shopping
Einkäufe machen	to do the shopping
ein Geschäft (*n*)	shop
ein Laden (*m*)	shop
eine Handlung	shop
billig	cheap
preiswert	inexpensive
günstig	good value
teuer	expensive
gratis	free
kostenlos	free
umsonst	for nothing, free
zum Mitnehmen	to take away
reduziert	reduced
heruntergesetzt	reduced
im Sonderangebot	on special offer
gebraucht	second-hand
ausverkauft	sold out
geöffnet	open
geschlossen	closed
ein Kunde, eine Kundin	customer
ein(e) Verkäufer(in)	shop assistant
der Umtausch	exchange

die Selbstbedienung	self-service
der Sonderpreis	special price
der Ausverkauf	clearance sale
der Sommerschlußverkauf	summer sales
der Winterschlußverkauf	winter sales
die Geschäftszeiten	opening times
die Öffnungszeiten	opening times

Geschäfte   shops

die Apotheke	dispensing chemist's
die Bäckerei	baker's
die Blumenhandlung	florist's
die Boutique	boutique
die Buchhandlung	bookshop
die chemische Reinigung	dry cleaner's
die Drogerie	chemist's
das Einkaufszentrum	shopping centre
die Eisenwarenhandlung	ironmonger's
der Feinkostladen	delicatessen
das Fischgeschäft	fishmonger's
die Fleischerei	butcher's
der Juwelierladen	jeweller's
das Kaufhaus	department store
der Kiosk	kiosk
die Konditorei	confectioner's and cake shop
das Kurzwarengeschäft	haberdasher's
das Lebensmittelgeschäft	grocer's
die Lederwarenhandlung	leather goods shop
der Markt	market
die Metzgerei	butcher's
das Milchgeschäft	dairy
die Obst- und Gemüsehandlung	greengrocer's
der Optiker	optician
das Reisebüro	travel agent's
das Schallplattengeschäft	record shop
der Schnellimbiß	take-away
die Schnellreinigung	(fast) dry cleaner's

die Schreibwarenhandlung	stationer's
der Schuhmacher	cobbler's
der Souvenirladen	souvenir shop
die Spielwarenhandlung	toy shop
das Sportgeschäft	sports shop
der Supermarkt	supermarket
der Süßwarenladen	confectioner's
der Tabakwarenladen	tobacconist's
die Tierhandlung	pet shop
das Warenhaus	department store
die Wäscherei	laundry
der Waschsalon	launderette
die Wein- und Spirituosenhandlung	off-licence
der Wochenmarkt	weekly market
der Zeitungsladen	newsagent's
ein Einkaufswagen (*m*)	(supermarket) trolley
ein Einkaufskorb (*m*)	shopping basket
eine Tasche	bag
eine Tüte	plastic/paper bag
eine Plastiktüte	plastic bag
die Einkäufe (*pl*)	shopping
eine Packung	packet
eine Dose	tin
eine Büchse	tin
die Theke	counter
der Ladentisch	counter
die Kasse	till
die Schlange	queue
der Preis	price
das Wechselgeld	(small) change
der Kassenzettel	receipt
ein Scheck (*m*)	cheque
eine Kreditkarte	credit card
die Abteilung	department
die Auswahl	selection, range
das Schaufenster	shop window
die Größe	size

| die Schuhgröße | shoe size |
| die Gebrauchsanweisung | instructions for use |

der Zucker ist alle
the sugar's all gone

ich gehe einkaufen
I'm going shopping

das ist aber günstig!
that's a bargain!

was darf es sein?
can I help you?

was für Brot haben Sie?
what sort of bread do you have?

ich hätte gern zwei Pfund Äpfel
I would like two pounds of apples please

sonst noch etwas?
anything else?

danke, das ist alles
that's all, thank you

wieviel macht das?
how much is it?

das macht zusammen 30 Mark
that comes to 30 marks

haben Sie das Geld passend?
have you got the exact change?

kann ich mit Scheck bezahlen?
can I pay by cheque?

soll ich es als Geschenk einpacken?
do you want it gift-wrapped?

ich mache gern einen Schaufensterbummel
I love window-shopping

See also Sections **2 CLOTHES, 10 JOBS AND WORK** *and* **31 MONEY**.

19. SPORT
SPORT

laufen	to run
joggen	to jog
schwimmen	to swim
tauchen	to dive
springen	to jump
werfen	to throw
Ski laufen/fahren	to ski
zum Skilaufen gehen	to go skiing
Rollschuh laufen	to skate
fischen	to fish
angeln	to fish
trainieren	to train
üben	to practise
sich trimmen	to get into shape
reiten	to ride
spielen	to play
Fußball/Volleyball spielen	to play football/volleyball
auf die Jagd gehen	to go hunting
ein Tor (*n*) schießen	to score a goal
gewinnen	to win
verlieren	to lose
in Führung sein	to be in the lead
schlagen	to beat
einen neuen Rekord aufstellen	to set up a new record
traben	to trot
galoppieren	to gallop
aufschlagen	to serve
schießen	to shoot
ein Profi (*m*)	professional
ein Amateur (*m*)	amateur

Sportarten

types of sport

der Sport	sport
das Aerobic	aerobics
der American Football	American football
das Angeln	fishing
das Badminton	badminton
der Basketball	basketball
das Bergsteigen	mountaineering
das Boxen	boxing
das Diskuswerfen	discus
das Drachenfliegen	hang-gliding
der Dreisprung	triple jump
das Eishockey	ice hockey
der Eiskunstlauf	figure skating
das Eisschießen	curling
das Fallschirmspringen	parachuting
das Fechten	fencing
der Federball	badminton
das Fischen	fishing
das Fitneßtraining	physical training
der Fußball	football
das Gewichtheben	weight-lifting
das Golf	golf
der Handball	handball
der Hochsprung	high jump
das Hockey	hockey
das Jagen	hunting
das Jogging	jogging
das Judo	judo
das Kanufahren	canoeing
das Karate	karate
das Kricket	cricket
das Kugelstoßen	putting the shot
das Laufen	running
die Leichtathletik	athletics
das Minigolf	minigolf
das Radfahren	cycling
das Reiten	horse riding

das Ringen	wrestling
das Rollschuhlaufen	roller skating
das Rudern	rowing
das Rugby	rugby
das Schießen	shooting
das Schlittschuhlaufen	skating
die Schwerathletik	weight-lifting, wrestling *etc*
das Schwimmen	swimming
das Segelfliegen	gliding
das Segeln	sailing
der Skilanglauf	cross-country skiing
das Skilaufen	skiing
das Speerwerfen	javelin
das Squash	squash
der Stabhochsprung	pole vault
das Tauchen	diving
das Tennis	tennis
das Tischtennis	table tennis
das Turnen	PE, gymnastics
der Volleyball	volleyball
das Wandern	rambling
der Wasserball	water polo
das Wasserski	water-skiing
der Weitsprung	long jump
das Windsurfen	windsurfing
der Wintersport	winter sports

Ausrüstung und Gerät

equipment

eine Angel(rute)	fishing rod
ein Ball (*m*)	ball
der Barren	parallel bars
Boxhandschuhe (*pl*)	boxing gloves
ein Fahrrad (*n*)	bicycle
ein Golfschläger (*m*)	golf club
ein Kanu (*n*)	canoe
eine Kugel	bowl, ball (*small*)
ein Netz (*n*)	net

ein **Ruderboot** (*n*)	rowing boat
ein **Sattel** (*m*)	saddle
ein **Schläger** (*m*)	bat
ein **Schnorchel** (*m*)	snorkel
Schwimmflossen (*pl*)	flippers, fins
ein **Segelboot** (*n*)	sailing boat
Skier (*pl*)	skis
Skistiefel (*pl*)	ski boots
ein **Skistock** (*m*)	ski pole
eine **Stoppuhr**	stopwatch
ein **Surfbrett** (*n*)	surfboard
eine **Taucherbrille**	goggles
ein **Tennisschläger** (*m*)	tennis racket

Sportstätten

places

ein **Fahrradweg** (*m*)	cycle track
ein **Freibad** (*n*)	open-air pool
ein **Golfplatz** (*m*)	golf course
ein **Hallenbad** (*n*)	indoor pool
der **Platz**	pitch, field, ground
der **Ring**	ring
eine **Schlittschuhbahn**	ice-rink
ein **Schwimmbad** (*n*)	swimming pool
der **Skilift**	skilift
eine **Skipiste**	(ski) slope
das **Spielfeld**	pitch
der **Sportplatz**	sports ground
ein **Sportzentrum** (*n*)	sports centre
ein **Stadion** (*n*)	stadium
ein **Tennisplatz** (*m*)	tennis court
der **Umkleideraum**	changing room

Wettbewerb

competing

das **Training**	training
ein **Team** (*n*)	team
eine **Mannschaft**	team
der **Sieger**, die **Siegerin**	winner

der Verlierer, die Verliererin	loser
ein Rennen (*n*)	race
eine Etappe	stage
ein Spurt (*n*)	sprint
ein Spiel (*n*)	match, game
die Halbzeit	half-time
ein Tor (*n*)	goal
der Spielstand	score
das Ergebnis	result
ein Unentschieden (*n*)	draw
die Verlängerung	extra time
der Elfmeter	penalty kick
das Elfmeterschießen	sudden death play-off
ein Marathonlauf (*m*)	marathon
ein Wettbewerb (*m*)	sports competition
die Meisterschaft	championship
ein Turnier (*n*)	tournament
das Viertelfinale	quarter finals
das Halbfinale	semi-finals
das Endspiel	final
das Finale	final
der Rekord	record
der Weltrekord	world record
die Weltmeisterschaft	world cup
die Olympischen Spiele	Olympic Games
die Bundesliga	German Football League
eine Medaille	medal
ein Pokal (*m*)	cup

Teilnehmer people

ein Sportler	sportsman
eine Sportlerin	sportswoman
ein Fußballspieler (*m*)	football player
der Torwart	goalkeeper
der Rechtsaußen	outside right
der Linksaußen	outside left
der Mittelstürmer	centre-forward
ein Verteidiger (*m*)	defender

ein **Mittelfeldspieler** (m)	mid-field player
ein **Stürmer** (m)	striker
der **Libero**	sweeper
ein(e) **Bergsteiger(in)**	mountaineer
ein(e) **Leichtathlet(in)**	athlete
ein **Boxer** (m)	boxer
ein(e) **Läufer(in)**	runner
ein **Radrennfahrer** (m)	racing cyclist
ein(e) **Radfahrer(in)**	cyclist
ein(e) **Tennisspieler(in)**	tennis player
ein(e) **Schlittschuhläufer(in)**	ice-skater
ein(e) **Eiskunstläufer(in)**	figure-skater
ein(e) **Taucher(in)**	diver
ein(e) **Skiläufer(in)**	skier
der **Schiedsrichter**	referee
der **Trainer**	manager
ein(e) **Meister(in)**	champion
ein(e) **Lehrer(in)**	instructor
ein(e) **Anhänger(in)**	supporter
ein(e) **Zuschauer(in)**	spectator
ein **Fan** (m)	fan

er treibt viel Sport
he does a lot of sport

die beiden Mannschaften haben unentschieden gespielt
the two teams drew

das Spiel mußte verlängert werden
they had to go into extra time

es steht eins zu null
the score is one-nil

auf die Plätze, fertig, los!
on your marks, get set, go

Achtung, fertig, los!
ready, steady, go!

See also Section **2 CLOTHES**.

20. FREIZEIT UND HOBBYS
LEISURE AND HOBBIES

sich interessieren für	to be interested in
sich amüsieren	to enjoy oneself
sich langweilen	to be bored
Zeit haben für	to have time for
lesen	to read
zeichnen	to draw
malen	to paint
bauen	to build
machen	to make
fotografieren	to take photographs, to photograph
sammeln	to collect
kochen	to cook
nähen	to sew
stricken	to knit
tanzen	to dance
singen	to sing
spielen	to play
teilnehmen an (+*dat*)	to take part in
gewinnen	to win
verlieren	to lose
schlagen	to beat
wetten	to bet
einsetzen	to stake
spazierengehen	to go for walks
bummeln	to stroll, to wander
klettern	to climb
eine Radtour machen	to go for a cycle ride
radfahren	to cycle
eine Fahrt mit dem Auto machen	to go for a run in the car
angeln gehen	to go fishing

interessant	interesting
spannend	exciting
faszinierend	fascinating
langweilig	boring
ein Hobby (*n*)	hobby
ein Zeitvertreib (*m*)	pastime
die Freizeit	free time
eine Freizeitbeschäftigung	pastime
ein Treffpunkt (*m*)	meeting place
ein Stammtisch (*m*)	table for regulars in a pub
ein Klub (*m*)	club
ein Verein (*m*)	club
ein Jugendklub (*m*)	youth club
die Pfadfinder (*pl*)	boy scouts, girl guides
ein Mitglied (*n*)	member (*male and female*)
das Lesen	reading
ein Buch (*n*)	book
ein Roman (*m*)	novel
ein Taschenbuch (*n*)	pocket book
ein Comic strip (*m*)	strip cartoon
eine Illustrierte	magazine
ein Magazin (*n*)	magazine
die Zeichnung	drawing
das Gemälde	painting
ein Pinsel (*m*)	brush
die Töpferei	pottery
das Heimwerken	DIY
der Modellbau	model-making
ein Hammer (*m*)	hammer
ein Schraubenzieher (*m*)	screwdriver
ein Nagel (*m*)	nail
eine Schraube	screw
ein Bohrer (*m*)	drill
eine Säge	saw
die Fotografie	photography
eine Kamera	camera

ein Fotoapparat (*m*)	camera
ein Film (*m*)	film
ein Foto (*n*)	photograph
ein Dia (*n*)	slide
eine Filmkamera	cine-camera
das Video	video
die Computertechnik	computing
ein Computer (*m*)	computer
Computerspiele (*pl*)	computer games
das Briefmarkensammeln	stamp collecting
eine Briefmarke	stamp
ein Album (*n*)	album, scrapbook
die Sammlung	collection
das Kochen	cooking
ein Rezept (*n*)	recipe
das Schneidern	dressmaking
die Handarbeit	needlework and knitting
die Nähmaschine	sewing machine
eine Nadel	needle
ein Faden (*m*)	thread
das Stricken	knitting
eine Stricknadel	knitting needle
das Tanzen	dancing
das Ballett	ballet
die Musik	music
die klassische Musik	classical music
die Popmusik	pop music
der Gesang	singing
ein Lied (*n*)	song
ein Schlager (*m*)	pop song, hit
ein Chor (*m*)	choir
das Klavier	piano
die Geige	violin
das Cello	cello
die Klarinette	clarinet
die Flöte	flute
die Blockflöte	recorder

eine Gitarre	guitar
das Schlagzeug	drums
ein Spiel (n)	game
ein Spielzeug (n)	toy
eine Puppe	doll
ein Brettspiel (n)	board game
das Schach	chess
das Damespiel	draughts
ein Puzzle (n)	jigsaw
Karten (pl)	cards
ein Kartenspiel (n)	game/deck of cards
ein Würfel (m)	dice
eine Wette	bet
ein Spaziergang	walk
eine Autofahrt	drive
eine Wanderung	ramble, hike
ein Ausflug (m)	excursion, outing
das Radfahren	cycling
das Fahrrad	bicycle
die Vogelbeobachtung	birdwatching
das Angeln	fishing

ich lese/stricke gern
I like reading/knitting

Klaus kann gut basteln
Klaus is very good with his hands

Erika ist eine begeisterte Kinogängerin
Erika is very keen on the cinema

ich spiele Klavier
I play the piano

du bist dran
it's your turn

See also Sections **19 SPORT, 21 MEDIA, 22 EVENINGS OUT**
and **43 CAMPING**.

21. DIE MEDIEN
THE MEDIA

hören	to listen to
sehen	to watch
fernsehen	to watch television
lesen	to read
einschalten	to switch on
anmachen	to switch on
ausschalten	to switch off
ausmachen	to switch off
umschalten	to switch over

Radio — radio

ein Radio (*n*)	radio
ein Transistorradio (*n*)	transistor
ein Walkman (*m*) (*R*)	walkman (*R*), personal stereo
eine (Radio)sendung	(radio) broadcast, programme
Nachrichten (*pl*)	news
ein Interview (*n*)	interview
der Rundfunk	radio
ein Rundfunkquiz (*n*)	radio quiz
die Hitparade	charts
eine Single	single
eine LP	LP
ein Werbespot (*m*)	commercial
ein(e) Zuhörer(in)	listener
der Empfang	reception
eine Störung	interference

Fernsehen — television

das Fernsehen	TV

der Fernseher	TV, television set
das Fernsehgerät	television (set)
der Fernsehapparat	television (set)
das Farbfernsehen	colour television
das Schwarzweißfernsehen	black and white television
eine Antenne	aerial
der Kanal	channel
das Programm	channel
eine Sendung	programme
ein Programm (n)	programme
eine Nachrichtensendung	news bulletin, newscast
die Fernsehnachrichten (pl)	television news
die Tagesschau	television news
ein Film (m)	film
ein Dokumentarbericht (m)	documentary
eine Fernsehserie	serial, soap opera
ein Werbespot (m)	commercial
eine Reklamesendung	commercial
ein(e) Nachrichten-sprecher(in)	newsreader, newscaster
ein(e) Ansager(in)	announcer
ein(e) Zuschauer(in)	viewer
das Kabelfernsehen	cable TV
ein Videorecorder (m)	video recorder

Presse   press

eine Zeitung	newspaper
eine Tageszeitung	daily paper
eine Morgen-/Abendzeitung	morning/evening paper
eine Wochenzeitung	weekly
eine Illustrierte	magazine
eine Zeitschrift	magazine
ein Nachrichtenmagazin (n)	news magazine
die Regenbogenpresse	gutter press
ein(e) Journalist(in)	journalist
ein(e) Reporter(in)	reporter
der Chefredakteur	chief editor
eine Reportage	press report

ein Artikel (*m*)	article
Schlagzeilen (*pl*)	headlines
eine Rubrik	(regular) column
der Sportteil	sports section
der Kummerkasten	agony column
die Reklame	advertisement, advertising
Kleinanzeigen (*pl*)	classified ads
eine Pressekonferenz	press conference
eine Nachrichtenagentur	news agency
die Auflage	circulation

auf Kurzwelle/Mittelwelle/Langwelle/UKW
on short/medium/long wave/FM

im Radio/Fernsehen
on the radio/on television

live aus Frankfurt
live from Frankfurt

was gibt es heute abend im Fernsehen?
what's on television tonight?

im zweiten Programm läuft ein Film
there's a film on channel 2

"wir schalten um nach Köln"
'we're going over to Cologne'

22. ABENDUNTERHALTUNG
EVENINGS OUT

ausgehen	to go out
tanzen	to dance
tanzen gehen	to go dancing
besuchen	to visit
einladen	to invite
geben	to give
reservieren	to book
applaudieren	to applaud
mitbringen	to bring
schenken	to give
begleiten	to accompany
bestellen	to order
empfehlen	to recommend
nach Hause gehen/kommen	to go/come home
allein	alone
zusammen	together

Veranstaltungen — shows

das Theater	theatre
ein Kostüm (*n*)	costume
die Bühne	stage
der Vorhang	curtain
die Garderobe	cloakroom
das Parkett	stalls
der erste Rang	dress circle
die Loge	box
die Galerie	gods
die Reihe	row
die Pause	interval
ein Programm (*n*)	programme
ein Stück (*n*)	play

ein Schauspiel (*n*)	play
eine Komödie	comedy
eine Tragödie	tragedy
eine Oper	opera
eine Operette	operetta
ein Musical (*n*)	musical
ein Ballett (*n*)	ballet
ein Konzert (*n*)	concert
ein Rockkonzert (*n*)	rock concert
eine Aufführung	show
eine Vorstellung	performance
das Orchester	orchestra
das Feuerwerk	fireworks
ein(e) Zuschauer(in)	member of the audience
das Publikum	audience
die Platzanweiserin	usherette
ein(e) Schauspieler(in)	actor/actress
ein(e) Tänzer(in)	dancer
der Dirigent	conductor
ein(e) Musiker(in)	musician

Kino — the cinema

ein (Spiel)film (*m*)	film
ein Kino (*n*)	cinema
die Kasse	ticket office
die Vorstellung	showing
eine (Eintritts)karte	ticket
die Leinwand	screen
der Projektor	projector
ein Zeichentrickfilm (*m*)	cartoon
ein Horrorfilm (*m*)	horror film
ein Science-fiction-Film (*m*)	science fiction film
ein Western (*m*)	Western
ein Kriminalfilm (*m*)	detective film
ein Krimi (*m*)	detective film
Untertitel (*pl*)	subtitles

ein(e) Regisseur(in)	director
ein(e) Filmemacher(in)	film-maker
ein Filmstar *(m)*	star *(male and female)*

Tanz und Diskotheken

dances and discos

ein Tanz *(m)*	dance
ein Tanzsaal *(m)*	dance hall
eine Diskothek	disco(theque)
ein Nachtklub *(m)*	night club
eine Bar	bar
eine (Schall)platte	record
die Tanzfläche	dance floor
der Rock	rock-and-roll
eine Popgruppe	pop group
der Diskjockey	DJ
ein(e) Sänger(in)	singer
der Rausschmeißer	bouncer

essen gehen

eating out

ein Restaurant *(n)*	restaurant
ein Café *(n)*	café
eine Gaststätte	restaurant
ein Lokal *(n)*	pub
eine Kneipe	pub, boozer
eine Wirtschaft	pub
eine Imbißstube	snack bar
ein Schnellimbiß *(m)*	fast food restaurant, take-away
ein(e) Kellner(in)	waiter/waitress
der Oberkellner	head waiter
die Speisekarte	menu
die Weinkarte	wine list
die Rechnung	bill
das Trinkgeld	tip

ein Chinarestaurant (*n*)	Chinese restaurant
ein italienisches Restaurant	Italian restaurant
ein griechisches Restaurant	Greek restaurant
eine Pizzeria	pizzeria

Einladungen   parties

eine Einladung	invitation
Gäste (*pl*)	guests
der Gastgeber	host
die Gastgeberin	hostess
ein Geschenk (*n*)	present
ein Drink (*m*)	drink
Erdnüsse (*pl*)	peanuts
Salzstangen (*pl*)	salt sticks
eine Party	party
eine Fete	party
eine Feier	celebration
der Geburtstag	birthday

Zugabe!
encore!

möchten Sie mit mir tanzen?
would you like to dance with me?

Herr Ober, ich möchte zahlen
waiter, can I pay please?

einschließlich/inklusive 10 Prozent Bedienung
10% service charge included

"Sonntags Ruhetag"
'closed on Sundays'

See also Section **16 FOOD**.

23. MEIN ZIMMER
MY ROOM

(an)klopfen	to knock
der (Fuß)boden	floor
der Teppich	carpet
der Teppichboden	fitted carpet
die Decke	ceiling
die Tür	door
das Fenster	window
Vorhänge (*pl*)	curtains
Fensterläden (*pl*)	shutters
Jalousien (*pl*)	blinds
die Tapete	wallpaper

Möbel — furniture

die Möbel (*pl*)	furniture
ein Möbelstück (*n*)	piece of furniture
das Bett	bed
die Bettdecke	cover
das Federbett	continental quilt
die Tagesdecke	bedspread
der Nachttisch	bedside table
die Kommode	chest of drawers
die Frisierkommode	dressing table
der Kleiderschrank	wardrobe
der Schrank	cupboard
eine Truhe	chest
der Schreibtisch	desk
ein Stuhl (*m*)	chair
ein Hocker (*m*)	stool
ein Sessel (*m*)	armchair
Regale (*pl*)	shelves
ein Bücherregal (*n*)	bookcase

Gegenstände	objects
eine Lampe	lamp
eine Nachttischlampe	bedside lamp
der Lampenschirm	lampshade
ein Wecker (*m*)	alarm clock
ein Radiowecker (*m*)	radio alarm
ein Läufer (*m*)	rug
ein Poster (*n*)	poster
ein Plakat (*n*)	poster
ein Bild (*n*)	picture
ein Foto (*n*)	photograph
ein Spiegel (*m*)	mirror
ein Buch (*n*)	book
eine Illustrierte	magazine
ein Comicheft (*n*)	comic
ein Tagebuch (*n*)	diary
ein Spiel (*n*)	game
ein Spielzeug (*n*)	toy

"herein!"
'come in!'

See also Sections **15 DAILY ROUTINE** *and* **24 THE HOUSE**.

24. DAS HAUS
THE HOUSE

wohnen	to live
heizen	to heat
umziehen	to move (house)
gelegen	situated
gemütlich	cosy, pleasant
die Miete	rent
die Hypothek	mortgage
ein(e) Mieter(in)	tenant
der Eigentümer	owner
der Hausmeister	caretaker
der Möbelpacker	removal man
ein Haus (*n*)	house
ein Einfamilienhaus (*n*)	detached house
ein Bungalow (*m*)	bungalow
eine Villa	villa
ein Reihenhaus (*n*)	terraced house
ein Doppelhaus (*n*)	semi-detached
eine Wohnung	flat
eine Sozialwohnung	council flat
ein Altbau (*m*)	old house
ein Neubau (*n*)	new house
der Wohnblock	block of flats
ein Apartment (*n*)	studio flat
eine möblierte Wohnung	furnished flat

Teile des Hauses — parts of the house

das Souterrain	basement
das Erdgeschoß	ground floor
das Obergeschoß	upper storey
der erste Stock	first floor
der Dachboden	loft

der Keller	cellar
ein Zimmer (*n*)	room
die Ecke	corner
der Stock	floor, storey
die Etage	floor, storey
der Flur	landing
das Treppenhaus	staircase
die Treppe	stairs
eine Stufe	step
das Geländer	bannisters
der Aufzug	lift
der Fahrstuhl	lift
eine Wand	wall
das Dach	roof
ein Dachziegel (*m*)	roof tile
der Kamin	chimney, fireplace
eine Tür	door
die Eingangstür	front door
ein Fenster (*n*)	window
der Balkon	balcony
der Garten	garden
der Vorgarten	front garden
die Terrasse	terrace
der Hof	yard
der Hinterhof	back yard
die Garage	garage
innen	inside
außen	outside
oben	upstairs
unten	downstairs

die Zimmer   the rooms

die Diele	entrance, hall
der Flur	landing
die Küche	kitchen
die Kochnische	kitchen recess
das Eßzimmer	dining room

das Wohnzimmer	living room, sitting room, lounge
das Arbeitszimmer	study
das Schlafzimmer	bedroom
das Badezimmer	bathroom
die Toilette	toilet
das Klo	loo
das WC	toilet
das Kinderzimmer	children's room

Möbel   furniture

eine Anrichte	dresser
ein Badezimmerschrank (*m*)	bathroom cabinet
ein Bücherregal (*n*)	bookcase
ein Kleiderschrank (*m*)	wardrobe
eine Liege	divan
Regale (*pl*)	shelves
ein Schaukelstuhl (*m*)	rocking chair
ein Schrank (*m*)	cupboard
ein Schreibtisch (*m*)	desk
ein Servierwagen (*m*)	trolley
ein Sessel (*m*)	armchair
ein Sideboard (*n*)	sideboard
ein Sofa (*n*)	sofa
ein Stuhl (*m*)	chair
ein Tisch (*m*)	table

das Bad	bath
die Dusche	shower
ein Waschbecken (*n*)	washbasin
ein Bidet (*n*)	bidet

Gegenstände und   objects and
Einrichtungen   fittings

ein Abfalleimer (*m*)	bin
eine Antenne	aerial

ein Aschenbecher (*m*)	ashtray
eine Bademotte	bathmat
eine Badewanne	bathtub
ein Bild (*n*)	picture
der Briefkasten	letterbox
ein Foto (*n*)	photograph
eine Fußmatte	doormat
die Garderobe	coat rack
die Gasheizung	gas heating
der Hahn	tap
der Heizkörper	radiator
die Heizung	heating
Kacheln (*pl*)	tiles
der Kamin	fireplace
eine Kerze	candle
ein Kerzenhalter (*m*)	candlestick
ein Kissen (*n*)	cushion
eine Klinke	door-handle
ein Kohleofen (*m*)	coal-burning stove
eine Lampe	lamp
ein Läufer (*m*)	rug
ein Papierkorb (*m*)	wastepaper basket
ein Poster (*n*)	poster
ein Rahmen (*m*)	frame
der Riegel	bolt
ein Schirmständer (*m*)	umbrella stand
ein Schlüssel (*m*)	key
das Schlüsselloch	keyhole
ein Spiegel (*m*)	mirror
die Spüle	kitchen sink
die Steckdose	socket
der Stecker	plug
eine Stehlampe	standard lamp
die Tapete	wallpaper
der Teppichboden	(fitted) carpet
ein Tisch (*m*)	table
die Türklingel	doorbell
eine Türklinke	door-handle
eine Vase	vase
Vorhänge (*pl*)	curtains

die Zentralheizung	central heating
der Zierat	ornament
Zimmerpflanzen (*pl*)	house plants
ein Transistorradio (*n*)	transistor
ein Radio (*n*)	radio
ein Plattenspieler (*m*)	record player
eine Stereoanlage	stereo
ein Tonbandgerät (*n*)	tape-recorder
ein Kassettenrecorder (*m*)	cassette recorder
eine (Schall)platte	record
eine Langspielplatte	long-playing record
eine LP	LP
eine Single	single
eine Maxi-Single	12″ single
eine Kassette	cassette
eine Compact-disc	compact disk
eine Schreibmaschine	typewriter
ein Computer (*m*)	computer
ein Videorecorder (*m*)	video (recorder)
eine Videokassette	video cassette

der Garten   the garden

der Rasen	lawn
das Gras	grass
Blumenbeete (*pl*)	flowerbeds
die Gartenmöbel (*pl*)	garden furniture
ein Sonnenschirm (*m*)	parasol
ein Rasenmäher (*m*)	lawnmower
eine Gießkanne	watering can
ein Schlauch (*m*)	hose

See also Sections **8 IDENTITY, 17 HOUSEWORK** *and* **23 MY ROOM**.

25. DIE STADT
THE CITY

eine Stadt	town, city
eine Großstadt	big city
eine Kleinstadt	small town
ein Dorf (n)	village
ein Ort (m)	place
ein Stadtteil (m)	district, part of town
eine Vorstadt	suburbs, outskirts
ein Vorort (m)	suburb
ein Bezirk (m)	area
ein Viertel (n)	district, part of town
das Industriegebiet	industrial area
die Wohngegend	residential district
die Altstadt	old town
die Stadtmitte	town/city centre
die City	city centre
die Umgebung	surroundings
eine Allee	avenue
eine Baustelle	building site
eine Fußgängerzone	pedestrian precinct
eine Gasse	narrow street
eine Geschäftsstraße	shopping street
die Hauptstraße	main road, high street
ein Kreisverkehr (m)	roundabout
ein Platz (m)	square
eine Sackgasse	cul-de-sac
eine Stadtautobahn	expressway
eine Straße	road, street
eine Umgehungsstraße	ring road
die Fahrbahn	road, roadway
der Bürgersteig	pavement
ein Parkplatz (m)	car park
ein Parkhaus (n)	multi-storey car park

eine Tiefgarage	underground car park
ein Park (*m*)	park
ein Friedhof (*m*)	cemetery
eine Brücke	bridge
der Marktplatz	market place
die Stadtmauer	city walls
der Hafen	harbour
der Flughafen	airport
der Bahnhof	railway station
ein Stadtplan (*m*)	street map

Gebäude   buildings

ein Haus (*n*)	house, building
ein Gebäude (*n*)	building
das Rathaus	town hall
der Gerichtshof	Law Courts
das Fremdenverkehrsbüro	tourist information office
das Verkehrsamt	tourist office
das Postamt	post office
die Post	post office
die Hauptpost	main post office
eine Bücherei	library
eine Polizeiwache	police station
das Polizeipräsidium	police headquarters
die Kaserne	barracks
die Feuerwache	fire station
das Fundbüro	lost property office
ein Gefängnis (*n*)	prison
eine Fabrik	factory
ein Bürogebäude (*n*)	office building
ein Krankenhaus (*n*)	hospital
das Jugendzentrum	youth centre
das Arbeitsamt	job centre, employment office
ein Hotel (*n*)	hotel
ein Theater (*n*)	theatre
ein Kino (*n*)	cinema
die Oper	opera (house)

ein Museum (*n*)	museum
eine Galerie	art gallery
ein Schloß (*n*)	castle
eine Burg	castle
ein Turm (*m*)	tower
eine Kathedrale	cathedral
eine Kirche	church
ein Dom (*m*)	cathedral
ein Kirchturm (*m*)	church tower, steeple
eine Synagoge	synagogue
ein Denkmal (*n*)	memorial, monument
ein Kriegerdenkmal (*n*)	war memorial
eine Statue	statue
ein Hochhaus (*n*)	high-rise building
ein Wolkenkratzer (*m*)	skyscraper
ein Brunnen (*m*)	fountain

Menschen people

ein(e) Städter(in)	city dweller
ein(e) Einwohner(in)	inhabitant
ein(e) Passant(in)	passer-by
ein(e) Verkehrsteilnehmer(in)	road-user
ein(e) Tourist(in)	tourist
ein Stadtstreicher (*m*)	tramp

sie wohnt in der Stadt/am Stadtrand
she lives in town/in the suburbs

wir gehen in die Stadt
we're going into town

die Stadt München
the city of Munich

See also Sections **18 SHOPPING, 22 EVENINGS OUT, 26 CARS, 41 PUBLIC TRANSPORT, 45 GEOGRAPHICAL TERMS** *and* **64 DIRECTIONS**.

26. AUTOS
CARS

fahren	to drive, to go (*car*)
sich anschnallen	to put one's seat belt on
starten	to start (up)
schneller fahren	to drive faster
langsamer fahren	to slow down
bremsen	to brake
beschleunigen	to accelerate
anhalten	to stop
parken	to park
abschließen	to lock
abbiegen	to turn off
überholen	to overtake
wenden	to do a U-turn
sich einordnen	to get in lane
das Licht einschalten	to switch on one's lights
das Licht ausschalten	to switch off one's lights
die Lichthupe betätigen	to flash one's headlights
überqueren	to cross, to go through
überprüfen	to check
Abstand halten	to keep one's distance
Vorfahrt gewähren (+*dat*)	to give way
Vorfahrt haben	to have right of way
hupen	to hoot
schleudern	to skid
abschleppen	to tow
reparieren	to repair
eine Panne haben	to break down
kein Benzin mehr haben	to have run out of petrol
volltanken	to fill up
ein Rad wechseln	to change a wheel
sich strafbar machen	to commit an offence
die Geschwindigkeits- beschränkung einhalten	to keep to the speed limit

die Geschwindigkeits-beschränkung überschreiten	to break the speed limit
eine rote Ampel überfahren	to jump a red light
ein Stoppschild nicht beachten	to ignore a stop sign
den Führerschein vorzeigen müssen	to have to show one's licence
langsam	slow
schnell	fast
obligatorisch	compulsory
erlaubt	allowed
gestattet	permitted
verboten	forbidden
untersagt	prohibited
gesperrt	closed off

Fahrzeuge — vehicles

ein Auto (*n*)	car
ein Wagen (*m*)	car
ein Pkw (*m*)	motorcar
ein Fahrzeug (*n*)	vehicle
ein Automatikwagen (*m*)	automatic
eine Klapperkiste	old banger
ein Gebrauchtwagen (*m*)	second-hand car
ein zwei-/vier-/fünftüriger Wagen (*m*)	two/four/five-door car
ein Kombi(wagen) (*m*)	estate car
eine Limousine	saloon
ein Rennauto (*n*)	racing car
ein Sportwagen (*m*)	sports car
ein Leihwagen (*m*)	rented car
ein Wagen (*m*) mit Rechtssteuerung	right-hand drive car
ein Wagen (*m*) mit Linkssteuerung	left-hand drive car
ein Kabriolett (*n*)	convertible
der Hubraum	c.c.
das Modell	model
das Fabrikat	make

ein Lastwagen (*m*)	lorry
ein Lkw (*m*)	lorry
ein Sattelschlepper (*m*)	articulated lorry
ein Lieferwagen (*m*)	van
ein Abschleppwagen (*m*)	breakdown lorry
ein Motorrad (*n*)	motorbike
ein Moped (*n*)	moped
ein Mofa (*n*)	small moped
ein Motorroller (*m*)	scooter
ein Campingwagen (*m*)	Dormobile (*R*)
ein Wohnwagen (*m*)	caravan
ein Anhänger (*m*)	trailer

Verkehrsteilnehmer   road users

der Fahrer, die Fahrerin	driver
ein(e) Autofahrer(in)	motorist
ein Verkehrsrowdy (*m*)	reckless driver
ein(e) Sonntagsfahrer(in)	Sunday driver
ein(e) Mitfahrer(in)	passenger
ein Lastwagenfahrer (*m*)	lorry-driver
ein Lkw-Fahrer (*m*)	lorry-driver
ein(e) Motorradfahrer(in)	motorcyclist
ein(e) Radfahrer(in)	cyclist
ein(e) Anhalter(in)	hitch-hiker
ein(e) Tramper(in)	hitch-hiker
ein(e) Fußgänger(in)	pedestrian

Autoteile   car parts

das Abblendlicht	lights
die Antenne	aerial
das Armaturenbrett	dashboard
ein Aufkleber (*m*)	sticker
der Auspuff	exhaust
das Autoradio	car radio
die Batterie	battery
die Benzinuhr	petrol gauge

der Blinker	indicator
Bremsen (*pl*)	brakes
der Choke	choke
der Dachgepäckträger	roof rack
der Ersatzreifen	spare wheel
ein Ersatzteil (*n*)	spare part
das Fenster	window
Gänge (*pl*)	gears
der erste Gang	first gear
der zweite Gang	second gear
der dritte Gang	third gear
der vierte Gang	fourth gear
der fünfte Gang	fifth gear, overdrive
der Rückwärtsgang	reverse
der Leerlauf	neutral
das Gaspedal	accelerator
der Geschwindigkeitsmesser	speedometer
das Getriebe	gears
die Handbremse	handbrake
das Heck	rear part of car
die Heckscheibe	rear window
die Hecktür	hatchback
die Heizung	heating
die Hupe	horn
die Karosserie	body
der Keilriemen	fanbelt
der Kofferraum	boot
ein Kotflügel (*m*)	wing
der Kühler	radiator
die Kupplung	clutch
das Lenkrad	steering wheel
der Motor	engine
die Motorhaube	bonnet
das Nummernschild	number plate
der Ölstandanzeiger	oil gauge
das Pedal	pedal
ein Rad (*n*)	wheel
eine Radkappe	hub cap
der Reifen	tyre
Rücklichter (*pl*)	rear lights

der Rücksitz	back seat
der Rückspiegel	(rearview) mirror
der Schalthebel	gear lever
ein Scheibenwischer (*m*)	windscreen wiper
das Schloß	lock
der Seitenspiegel	wing mirror
der Sicherheitsgurt	seat belt
das Standlicht	sidelights
die Stoßstange	bumper
der Tank	tank
die Tür	door
die Übersetzung	transmission
das Verdeck	hood, soft top
der Vergaser	carburettor
der Vordersitz	front seat
der Wagenheber	jack
die Windschutzscheibe	windscreen
die Zündkerze	spark plug
die Zündung	ignition
das Benzin	petrol
das Normalbenzin	two-star (petrol)
das Super(benzin)	four-star (petrol)
der Kraftstoff	fuel
das bleifreie Benzin	unleaded petrol
das Diesel	diesel
das Öl	oil
das Frostschutzmittel	antifreeze

Schwierigkeiten   problems

die Reparatur	repair
eine (Reparatur)werkstatt	garage
eine Tankstelle	petrol station
eine SB-Tankstelle	self-service petrol station
die Zapfsäule	petrol pump
der Kfz-Mechaniker	car mechanic
der Tankwart	petrol pump attendant
die Versicherung	insurance
die Versicherungspolice	insurance policy

der Führerschein	driving licence
der Fahrzeugbrief	log book
der Fahrzeugschein	registration document
die grüne Karte	green card (*insurance*)
die Straßenverkehrsordnung	Highway Code
die Geschwindigkeit	speed
die Höchstgeschwindigkeit	maximum speed
die Geschwindigkeits- überschreitung	speeding
ein Vergehen (*n*)	offence
ein Strafzettel (*m*)	parking ticket
eine Geldbuße	fine
die Vorfahrt	right of way
das Parkverbot	no parking (area)
ein Parkschein (*m*)	car park ticket
das Halteverbot	no waiting (area)
eine Einfahrt	entrance
eine Zufahrt	drive (*in front of house*)
die Reifenpanne	flat tyre
die Panne	breakdown
ein Stau (*m*)	traffic jam
die Umleitung	diversion
die Straßenbauarbeiten (*pl*)	roadworks
das Glatteis	black ice
ein Loch (*n*)	(pot)hole
die Sicht	visibility
die Autowäsche	car wash
eine Waschstraße	car wash

Straßenführung   routes

der Verkehr	traffic
der Durchgangsverkehr	through traffic
die Straßenkarte	road map
die Straße	road
die Hauptverkehrsstraße	main road
die Nebenstraße	B road
eine Autobahn	motorway
eine Landstraße	B road, country road

der Bürgersteig	pavement
eine Einbahnstraße	one-way street
ein Stoppschild (n)	stop sign
ein Fußgängerüberweg (m)	pedestrian crossing
die Kurve	bend
die Kreuzung	crossroads
ein Autobahnkreuz (n)	motorway intersection
ein Autobahndreieck (n)	motorway junction
der Kreisverkehr	roundabout
die Spur	lane
der Mittelstreifen	central reservation
eine Überführung	fly-over
die Ausfahrt	exit
die Umgehungsstraße	bypass
die Ampel	traffic lights
die Gebühr	toll
eine Raststätte	service area
ein Rasthof (m)	service area
ein Verkehrszeichen (n)	road sign
ein Bahnübergang (m)	level crossing
eine Fußgängerbrücke	footbridge
ein Fußgängertunnel (m)	pedestrian underpass
eine Parkuhr	parking meter
ein Parkplatz (m)	parking place
ein Parkhaus (n)	multi-storey car park
ein Verkehrspolizist (m)	traffic policeman
ein Schülerlotse (m)	lollipop man/lady

welches Fabrikat ist es? – es ist ein Volkswagen
what make is it? – it's a Volkswagen

volltanken bitte
fill her up please

der Motor ist kaputt
the engine's had it

schalten Sie in den dritten Gang!
change into third gear!

er hat abgeblendet/auf Standlicht umgeschaltet
he dipped his headlights/switched to sidelights

sie fuhr 100 Kilometer in der Stunde
she was doing 62 miles an hour

in England fährt man links
in England they drive on the left

dieses Auto verbraucht . . . auf 100 Kilometer
this car does a 100 kilometres to . . . litres (. . . miles to the gallon)

ihm ist der Führerschein entzogen worden
he lost his driving licence

Sie haben sich verfahren
you've gone the wrong way

ich habe mich verfahren
I'm lost

fahren Sie bis zur dritten Querstraße rechts
drive on to the third turning on the right

bei Rot/Gelb/Grün
when the lights are/were red/amber/green

bei Rot durchfahren
to jump the lights

"Anlieger frei"
'residents only'

"Einfahrt/Ausfahrt freihalten"
'do not obstruct entrance/exit'

"Selbsttanken"
'self-service'

"Schritt fahren"
'drive at walking speed'

See also Section **51 ACCIDENTS**.

27. DIE NATUR
NATURE

die Landschaft — landscape

das Land	countryside
ein Feld (*n*)	field
eine Wiese	meadow
ein Wald (*m*)	forest, wood
eine Lichtung	clearing
ein Obstgarten (*m*)	orchard
ein Gebirge (*n*)	mountains
die Heide	heath
das Moor	moor
ein Sumpf (*m*)	marsh
ein Tal (*n*)	valley
eine Wüste	desert
der Dschungel	jungle
die Landwirtschaft	agriculture

Pflanzen — plants

wachsen	to grow
eine Pflanze	plant
ein Baum (*m*)	tree
ein Strauch (*m*)	shrub
ein Busch (*m*)	bush
die Wurzel	root
der Stamm	trunk
ein Ast (*m*)	branch
ein Zweig (*m*)	twig
eine Knospe	bud
eine Blume	flower
eine Blüte	blossom
ein Blatt (*n*)	leaf

das Laub	foliage
die Rinde	bark
der Wipfel	treetop
ein Tannenzapfen (*m*)	fir cone
ein Kiefernzapfen (*m*)	pine cone
eine Kastanie	horse chestnut
eine Eichel	acorn
eine Beere	berry
Algen (*pl*)	seaweed
das Heidekraut	heather
ein Pilz (*m*)	mushroom
der Farn	ferns
das Gras	grass
die Mistel	mistletoe
die Stechpalme	holly
der Efeu	ivy
das Unkraut	weeds
das Moos	moss
der Rhododendron	rhododendron
das Schilf	reeds
der Klee	clover
der Weinstock	vine

Bäume   trees

ein Laubbaum (*m*)	deciduous tree
ein Nadelbaum (*m*)	conifer
ein Ahorn (*m*)	maple tree
eine Birke	birch
eine Buche	beech
eine Eibe	yew tree
eine Eiche	oak tree
eine Esche	ash tree
eine Kastanie	chestnut tree
eine Kiefer	pine tree
eine Pappel	poplar
eine Roßkastanie	horse chestnut tree
eine Tanne	fir tree

eine Trauerweide	weeping willow
eine Ulme	elm

Obstbäume — fruit trees

ein Aprikosenbaum (*m*)	apricot tree
ein Kirschbaum (*m*)	cherry tree
ein Birnbaum (*m*)	pear tree
ein Apfelbaum (*m*)	apple tree
ein Pflaumenbaum (*m*)	plum tree

Blumen — flowers

der Stiel	stem
die Blüte	blossom
ein Blütenblatt (*n*)	petal
der Pollen	pollen
eine Anemone	anemone
eine Butterblume	buttercup
eine Chrysantheme	chrysanthemum
der Flieder	lilac
ein Gänseblümchen (*n*)	daisy
die Gartenwicke	sweetpeas
das Geißblatt	honeysuckle
eine Geranie	geranium
eine Hyazinthe	hyacinth
die Iris	iris
der Jasmin	jasmine
eine Kornblume	cornflower
ein Krokus (*m*)	crocus
der Löwenzahn	dandelion
das Maiglöckchen	lily of the valley
eine Mohnblume	poppy
eine Nelke	carnation
eine Orchidee	orchid
eine Osterglocke	daffodil
eine Petunie	petunia
eine Primel	primrose, primula

eine Rose	rose
ein Schneeglöckchen (*n*)	snowdrop
ein Stiefmütterchen (*n*)	pansy
eine Tulpe	tulip
ein Veilchen (*n*)	violet
ein Vergißmeinnicht (*n*)	forget-me-not
der Weißdorn	hawthorn

Haustiere — pets

bellen	to bark
miauen	to miaow
fressen	to eat
das Futter	food
das Hundefutter	dog food
ein Tier (*n*)	animal
ein Haustier (*n*)	pet
eine Katze	cat
ein Kater (*m*)	tom cat
ein Hund (*m*)	dog
ein Meerschweinchen (*n*)	guinea pig
ein Hamster (*m*)	hamster
ein Goldfisch (*m*)	goldfish
ein Wellensittich (*m*)	budgerigar
ein Kanarienvogel (*m*)	canary
eine Schildkröte	tortoise

Tiere auf dem Bauernhof — farm animals

das Vieh	cattle
ein Bulle (*m*)	bull
eine Ente	duck
ein Esel (*m*)	donkey
eine Gans	goose
ein Hahn (*m*)	cock
ein Huhn (*n*)	chicken, hen

ein Kalb (n)	calf
ein Kaninchen (n)	rabbit
eine Kuh	cow
ein Küken (n)	chick
ein Lamm (n)	lamb
ein Maultier (n)	mule
ein Ochse (m)	ox
ein Pferd (n)	horse
ein Schaf (n)	sheep
ein Schafbock (m)	ram
ein Schwein (n)	pig
ein Truthahn (m)	turkey
eine Ziege	nanny-goat
ein Ziegenbock (m)	billy-goat

wilde Tiere

wild animals

ein Säugetier (n)	mammal
ein Fisch (m)	fish
Reptilien (pl)	reptiles
ein Bein (n)	leg
eine Pfote	paw
das Maul	mouth
der Schwanz	tail
der Rüssel	trunk
die Schnauze	muzzle, snout
Krallen (pl)	claws
Hörner (pl)	horns
das Fell	skin, fur
der Pelz	fur
ein Zoo (m)	zoo
ein Tierpark (m)	zoo
ein Käfig (m)	cage
ein Affe (m)	monkey
eine Antilope	antelope
ein Bär (m)	bear
ein Biber (m)	beaver
ein Büffel (m)	buffalo

ein Delphin (*m*)	dolphin
ein Eber (*m*)	boar
ein Eichhörnchen (*n*)	squirrel
ein Elefant (*m*)	elephant
eine Feldmaus	fieldmouse
ein Fuchs (*m*)	fox
eine Giraffe	giraffe
ein Gorilla (*m*)	gorilla
ein Hai (*m*)	shark
ein Hase (*m*)	hare
ein Hirsch (*m*)	stag
ein Igel (*m*)	hedgehog
ein Kamel (*n*)	camel
ein Känguruh (*n*)	kangaroo
ein Koalabär (*m*)	koala bear
ein Leopard (*m*)	leopard
ein Löwe, eine Löwin	lion
eine Maus	mouse
ein Nashorn (*n*)	rhinoceros
ein Nilpferd (*n*)	hippopotamus
eine Ratte	rat
ein Reh (*n*)	doe
eine Robbe	seal
eine Schildkröte	tortoise
ein Tiger (*m*)	tiger
ein Tintenfisch (*m*)	octopus
ein Wal (*m*)	whale
eine Wasserschildkröte	turtle
ein Wiesel (*n*)	weasel
ein Wildpferd (*n*)	wild horse
ein Wolf, eine Wölfin	wolf
ein Zebra (*n*)	zebra

Reptilien   reptiles

ein Krokodil (*n*)	crocodile
ein Alligator (*m*)	alligator
eine Eidechse	lizard
eine Schlange	snake

eine Klapperschlange	rattlesnake
eine Otter	adder
eine Ringelnatter	grass snake
eine Kobra	cobra
eine Boa	boa
eine Blindschleiche	slow-worm
ein Frosch (*m*)	frog
eine Kröte	toad
eine Kaulquappe	tadpole

Vögel — birds

ein Vogel (*m*)	bird
ein Raubvogel (*m*)	bird of prey
der Fuß	foot
Krallen (*pl*)	claws
Klauen (*pl*)	claws
der Flügel	wing
der Schnabel	beak
eine Feder	feather
ein Adler (*m*)	eagle
eine Amsel	blackbird
eine Blaumeise	blue tit
ein Buchfink (*m*)	chaffinch
eine Drossel	thrush
eine Elster	magpie
eine Eule	owl
ein Falke (*m*)	falcon
ein Fasan (*m*)	pheasant
ein Fink (*m*)	finch
ein Flamingo (*m*)	flamingo
ein Geier (*m*)	vulture
eine Krähe	crow
ein Kuckuck (*m*)	cuckoo
eine Lerche	lark
eine Meise	(blue) tit
eine Möwe	seagull
eine Nachtigall	nightingale
ein Papagei (*m*)	parrot

ein Pfau (*m*)	peacock
ein Pinguin (*m*)	penguin
ein Reiher (*m*)	heron
ein Rotkehlchen (*n*)	robin
eine Schwalbe	swallow
ein Schwan (*m*)	swan
ein Spatz (*m*)	sparrow
ein Star (*m*)	starling
ein Storch (*m*)	stork
ein Strauß (*m*)	ostrich
eine Taube	dove, pigeon
ein Uhu (*m*)	owl

Insekten   insects

eine Ameise	ant
eine Biene	bee
eine Fliege	fly
eine Heuschrecke	grasshopper
eine Hummel	bumblebee
eine Küchenschabe	cockroach
ein Marienkäfer (*m*)	ladybird
eine Motte	moth
eine Mücke	gnat
eine Raupe	caterpillar
ein Schmetterling (*m*)	butterfly
eine Schnake	daddy-long-legs
eine Spinne	spider
eine Stechmücke	gnat, midge
eine Stubenfliege	housefly
eine Wespe	wasp

See also Sections **16 FOOD, 44 SEASIDE** *and* **45 GEOGRAPHICAL TERMS**.

28. WIE IST DAS WETTER?
WHAT'S THE WEATHER LIKE?

regnen	to rain
nieseln	to drizzle
schneien	to snow
frieren	to be freezing
tauen	to thaw
wehen	to blow
scheinen	to shine
schmelzen	to melt
sich verschlechtern	to get worse
sich verbessern	to improve
sich ändern	to change
bedeckt	overcast
wolkig	cloudy
klar	clear
sonnig	sunny
heiter	fine
regnerisch	rainy
neblig	misty, foggy
trüb	dull
stürmisch	stormy
schwül	muggy
trocken	dry
warm	warm
heiß	hot
kalt	cold
mild	mild
angenehm	pleasant
furchtbar	awful
veränderlich	changeable
in der Sonne	in the sun
im Schatten	in the shade
das Wetter	weather
die Temperatur	temperature

die Höchsttemperatur	maximum temperature
die Tiefsttemperatur	minimum temperature
die Meteorologie	meteorology
die Wettervorhersage	weather forecast
der Wetterbericht	weather forecast
das Klima	climate
die Atmosphäre	atmosphere
die Luft	air
der Luftdruck	atmospheric pressure
eine Verbesserung	improvement
eine Veränderung	change
das Thermometer	thermometer
ein Grad (n)	degree
das Barometer	barometer
der Himmel	sky

Regen   rain

die Feuchtigkeit	humidity, dampness
der Niederschlag	precipitation
der Regen	rain
ein Regentropfen (m)	raindrop
eine Pfütze	puddle
eine Wolke	cloud
eine Wolkenschicht	cloud layer
ein Schauer (m)	shower
der Tau	dew
der Nieselregen	drizzle
der Nebel	fog, mist
der Hagel	hail
ein Hagelkorn (n)	hailstone
ein Wolkenbruch (m)	downpour
ein Dauerregen (m)	continuous rainfall
eine Überschwemmung	flood
ein Gewitter (n)	thunderstorm
der Donner	thunder
der Blitz	(flash of) lightning
eine Aufheiterung	sunny interval
ein Regenbogen (m)	rainbow

Kälte   cold weather

der Schnee	snow
eine Schneeflocke	snowflake
der Schneefall	snowfall
ein Schneesturm (*m*)	snowstorm
eine Lawine	avalanche
ein Schneeball (*m*)	snowball
ein Schneepflug (*m*)	snowplough
ein Schneemann (*m*)	snowman
der Frost	frost
das Tauwetter	thaw
der Rauhreif	(hoar)frost
das Glatteis	(black) ice
das Eis	ice
ein Eiszapfen (*m*)	icicle

schönes Wetter   good weather

die Sonne	sun
der Sonnenschein	sunshine
ein Sonnenstrahl (*m*)	ray of sunshine
die Hitze	heat
eine Hitzewelle	heatwave
die Trockenheit	dryness
die Dürre	drought

Wind   wind

der Wind	wind
ein Luftzug (*m*)	draught
eine Bö	gust of wind
eine Brise	breeze
ein Orkan (*m*)	hurricane
ein Tornado (*m*)	tornado
ein Sturm (*m*)	storm

es ist gutes/schlechtes Wetter
the weather is good/bad

es ist dreißig Grad im Schatten
the temperature is 30 in the shade

es ist minus zehn Grad (Celsius)
it's minus 10 degrees (Celsius)

es regnet immer noch
it's still raining

es regnet (Bindfäden)
it's raining (cats and dogs)

es schüttet
it's pouring

es schneit
it's snowing

es ist sonnig/neblig/regnerisch
it's sunny/foggy/rainy

mir ist eiskalt
I'm freezing cold

ich schwitze
I'm roasting

die Sonne scheint
the sun's shining

es donnert
it's thundering

es blitzt
there's lightning

morgen wird es regnen
it's going to rain tomorrow

bei diesem Sauwetter
in this atrocious weather

bei Regen
when it's raining

29. FAMILIE UND BEKANNTENKREIS
FAMILY AND FRIENDS

verwandt sein mit	to be related to
kennen	to know
gut auskommen (mit)	to get on well (with)
sich duzen	to use the 'du' form
sich siezen	to use the 'Sie' form

die Familie — the family

ein Familienmitglied (*n*)	member of the family
Eltern (*pl*)	parents
die Mutter	mother
der Vater	father
die Mutti	mum
der Vati	dad
das Kind	child
das Baby	baby
die Tochter	daughter
der Sohn	son
die Adoptivtochter	adopted daughter
der Adoptivsohn	adopted son
die Schwester	sister
die Zwillingsschwester	twin sister
der Bruder	brother
der Zwillingsbruder	twin brother
die Großmutter	grandmother
der Großvater	grandfather
die Oma	granny
der Opa	grandad
Großeltern (*pl*)	grandparents
Enkelkinder (*pl*)	grandchildren
die Enkelin	granddaughter
der Enkel	grandson
die Urgroßmutter	great-grandmother

der Urgroßvater	great-grandfather
die Frau	wife, woman
die Ehefrau	wife
der Mann	man, husband
der Ehemann	husband
ein Ehepaar (*n*)	married couple
die Verlobte	fiancée
der Verlobte	fiancé
der Schwager	brother-in-law
die Schwägerin	sister-in-law
die Schwiegermutter	mother-in-law
der Schwiegervater	father-in-law
Schwiegereltern (*pl*)	parents-in-law
die Schwiegertochter	daughter-in-law
der Schwiegersohn	son-in-law
die Tante	aunt
der Onkel	uncle
die Kusine/Cousine	cousin (*female*)
der Cousin	cousin (*male*)
der Vetter	cousin (*male*)
die Nichte	niece
der Neffe	nephew
die Patin	godmother
der Pate	godfather
die Patentochter	goddaughter
der Patensohn	godson
die Stiefmutter	stepmother
der Stiefvater	stepfather
die Stieftochter	stepdaughter
der Stiefsohn	stepson

Freunde und Bekannte

friends

Leute (*pl*)	people
der Freund	friend, boyfriend
die Freundin	friend, girlfriend
ein Bekannter, eine Bekannte	acquaintance, friend
der Bekanntenkreis	circle of friends

der Nachbar   neighbour (*male*)
die Nachbarin   neighbour (*female*)

hast du Geschwister?
have you got any brothers and sisters?

ich habe keine Geschwister
I have no brothers or sisters

ich bin ein Einzelkind
I'm an only child

meine Mutter erwartet ein Kind
my mother is expecting a baby

ich bin der/die älteste
I am the oldest

mein großer Bruder ist 17
my big brother is 17

meine älteste Schwester ist Friseuse
my eldest sister is a hairdresser

ich kümmere mich um meine kleine Schwester
I'm looking after my little sister

mein jüngster Bruder lutscht am Daumen
my youngest brother sucks his thumb

du bist mein bester Freund, Michael
you are my best friend, Michael

Monika ist meine beste Freundin
Monika is my best friend

er ist das schwarze Schaf in der Familie
he's the black sheep of the family

im engsten Familienkreis
with just the immediate family

See also Section **8 IDENTITY**.

30. SCHULE UND AUSBILDUNG
SCHOOL AND EDUCATION

zur Schule gehen	to go to school
studieren	to study
lernen	to learn
auswendig lernen	to learn by heart
die Hausaufgaben machen	to do one's homework
ein Gedicht aufsagen	to recite a poem
fragen	to ask
antworten	to answer
prüfen	to examine
aufpassen	to pay attention
sich melden	to put one's hand up
wissen	to know
wiederholen	to revise
eine Frage stellen	to ask a question
eine Prüfung machen	to sit an exam
seine Prüfung bestehen	to pass one's exams
seine Prüfung nicht bestehen	to fail one's exams
bei einer Prüfung durchfallen	to fail an exam
sitzenbleiben	to repeat a year, to stay down
verweisen	to expel, to suspend
bestrafen	to punish
die Schule schwänzen	to play truant
abwesend	absent
anwesend	present
gewissenhaft	conscientious
fleißig	hard-working
unaufmerksam	inattentive
undiszipliniert	undisciplined
begabt	gifted, talented
unbegabt	untalented
der Kindergarten	nursery school
die Grundschule	primary school
die Hauptschule	secondary school (10-14)

das Gymnasium	secondary school (10-18)
die Realschule	secondary school (10-16)
eine Gesamtschule	comprehensive
die Handelsschule	commercial school
ein Internat (*n*)	boarding school
die Universität	university
die Uni	university
die Technische Hochschule	polytechnic

in der Schule — at school

eine Klasse	class
das Klassenzimmer	classroom
die Schulleitung	headteacher's office
das Lehrerzimmer	staff room
die Bibliothek	library
das Labor	laboratory
das Sprachlabor	language lab
der Schulhof	playground
der Gang	corridor
die Aula	assembly hall
die Turnhalle	gym(nasium)

das Klassenzimmer — the classroom

ein Tisch (*m*)	desk, table
das Klassenbuch	class register
der Lehrertisch	teacher's desk
ein Stuhl (*m*)	chair
ein Schrank (*m*)	cupboard
die Tafel	blackboard
das Pult	desk, lectern
die Kreide	chalk
ein Schwamm (*m*)	sponge, duster
eine Schultasche	school-bag, satchel
eine Mappe	briefcase
ein Heft (*n*)	exercise book
ein Buch (*n*)	book

ein Schulbuch (n)	school book
ein Wörterbuch (n)	dictionary
ein Federmäppchen (n)	pencilcase
ein Kugelschreiber (m)	ballpoint pen, biro
ein Füller (m)	(fountain) pen
ein Bleistift (m)	pencil
ein Filzstift (m)	felt-tip pen
ein Bleistiftspitzer (m)	pencil sharpener
ein Radiergummi (n)	rubber
ein Lineal (n)	ruler
ein Zirkel (m)	pair of compasses
ein Geo-Dreieck (n)	set-square
ein Taschenrechner (m)	pocket calculator
ein Computer (m)	computer

Turnen   PE

Ringe (pl)	rings
das Seil	rope
der Barren	parallel bars
das Reck	horizontal bar
das Pferd	horse
das Netz	net
der Ball	ball

Lehrer und Schüler   teachers and pupils

ein(e) Grundschullehrer(in)	primary school teacher
der Lehrer	teacher (*man*)
die Lehrerin	teacher (*woman*)
der Direktor	headmaster
die Direktorin	headmistress
der Rektor	headteacher (*in a primary school*)
der Klassenlehrer	class teacher
der Deutschlehrer	German teacher
der Englischlehrer	English teacher
der Mathematiklehrer	maths teacher

ein Schulrat, eine Schulrätin	inspector
ein(e) Schüler(in)	pupil
ein(e) Gymnasiast(in)	secondary school pupil
ein(e) Student(in)	student
der Klassensprecher	class spokesperson
ein(e) Schulfreund(in)	schoolfriend

der Unterricht   teaching

das Schuljahr	school year
der Stundenplan	timetable
ein Fach (n)	subject
ein Wahlfach (n)	optional subject
ein Pflichtfach (n)	compulsory subject
das Lieblingsfach	favourite subject
eine Stunde	lesson
ein Kurs (m)	class, course
der Deutschunterricht	German class
der Mathematikunterricht	maths class
der Musikunterricht	music class
die Leistung	performance
der Fortschritt	progress
die Vokabeln (pl)	vocabulary
die Grammatik	grammar
die Rechtschreibung	spelling
das Schreiben	writing
das Lesen	reading
ein Gedicht (n)	poem

die Mathematik	mathematics
Mathe	maths
die Algebra	algebra
das Rechnen	arithmetic
die Geometrie	geometry
eine Addition	sum
eine Subtraktion	subtraction
eine Multiplikation	multiplication
eine Division	division
eine Gleichung	equation
ein Kreis (m)	circle

ein Dreieck (n)	triangle
ein Quadrat (n)	square
ein Rechteck (n)	rectangle
ein Winkel (m)	angle
ein rechter Winkel	right angle
die Oberfläche	surface
das Volumen	volume
der Durchmesser	diameter
der Umfang	circumference
die Geschichte	history
die Erdkunde	geography
die Naturwissenschaft	science
die Biologie	biology
die Chemie	chemistry
die Physik	physics
(neuere) Sprachen (pl)	(modern) languages
Deutsch	German
ein Aufsatz (m)	essay
eine Übersetzung	translation
die Musik	music
die Kunst	art
das Zeichnen	drawing
das Werken	handicrafts
der Sportunterricht	physical education, PE
Hausaufgaben (pl)	homework
eine Aufgabe	exercise
eine Strafarbeit	punishment, lines, imposition
eine Frage	question
die Antwort	answer
eine schriftliche Prüfung	written test
eine mündliche Prüfung	oral test
eine Klassenarbeit	test
ein Examen (n)	exam(ination)
ein Fehler (m)	mistake
eine gute Note	good mark
eine schlechte Note	bad mark
das Ergebnis	result

das Zeugnis	report
ein Preis (*m*)	prize
sehr gut	very good
gut	good
befriedigend	fair
ausreichend	satisfactory
mangelhaft	poor
ungenügend	unsatisfactory
das (Abschluß)zeugnis	certificate
ein Diplom (*n*)	diploma
das Abitur	A levels
die mittlere Reife	O levels
die Disziplin	discipline
eine Strafe	punishment
das Nachsitzen	detention
die Pause	break
die Klingel	bell
die Schulferien (*pl*)	school holidays
die Sommerferien (*pl*)	summer holidays
die großen Ferien (*pl*)	summer holidays
die Osterferien (*pl*)	Easter holidays
die Weihnachtsferien (*pl*)	Christmas holidays
eine Klassenfahrt	school trip

einen Schüler nachsitzen lassen
to give a pupil detention

er mußte nachsitzen
he was kept in

es hat geklingelt
the bell has gone

wir haben heute schulfrei
we've got no school today

was hast du heute auf?
what have you got for homework today?

er bekommt Nachhilfe in Englisch
he's getting extra tuition in English

31. GELD
MONEY

kaufen	to buy
verkaufen	to sell
ausgeben	to spend
leihen	to borrow
(ver)leihen	to lend
(be)zahlen	to pay
bar zahlen	to pay cash
mit Scheck bezahlen	to pay by cheque
einen Scheck einlösen	to cash a cheque
zurückzahlen	to pay back
wechseln	to change
auf Raten kaufen	to buy on HP
Kredit gewähren	to give credit
Geld abheben	to withdraw money
Geld einzahlen	to pay in money
Geld einwerfen	to insert money
sparen	to save money
abrechnen	to do one's accounts
Schulden haben	to have debts
reich	rich
arm	poor
pleite	broke
ein(e) Millionär(in)	millionaire
das Geld	money
das Taschengeld	pocket money
das Bargeld	cash
das Kleingeld	small change
ein Geldschein (*m*)	banknote
eine Münze	coin
ein Portemonnaie (*n*)	purse
eine Brieftasche	wallet
eine Zahlung	payment
Ausgaben (*pl*)	expenses
Ersparnisse (*pl*)	savings

eine Bank	bank
eine Sparkasse	savings bank
ein Postamt (*n*)	post office
eine Wechselstube	bureau de change
der Wechselkurs	exchange rate
die Kasse	till, cashdesk
der Schalter	counter
ein Geldautomat (*m*)	cash dispenser
ein Bankkonto (*n*)	bank account
ein Girokonto (*n*)	current account
ein Sparkonto (*n*)	savings account, deposit account
ein Postscheckkonto (*n*)	giro account
eine Abhebung	withdrawal
eine Überweisung	transfer
eine Kreditkarte	credit card
eine Scheckkarte	cheque card
ein Scheckheft (*n*)	chequebook
ein Scheck (*m*)	cheque
ein Reisescheck (*m*)	traveller's cheque
ein Euroscheck (*m*)	Eurocheque
ein Formular (*n*)	form
eine Postanweisung	postal order
ein Kredit (*m*)	credit
Schulden (*pl*)	debts
ein Darlehen (*n*)	loan
eine Hypothek	mortgage
die Währung	currency (*of a country*)
die Börse	Stock Exchange
eine Aktie	share
die Inflation	inflation
die Lebenshaltungskosten	cost of living
der Etat	budget
eine Mark	German mark
eine D-Mark	German mark
ein Markstück (*n*)	one-mark piece
ein Groschen (*m*)	10 pfennigs

31 GELD

ein Pfennig (*m*)	pfennig (*¹/₁₀₀ of a mark*)
ein Schilling (*m*)	(Austrian) shilling
ein Pfund (*n*) (**Sterling**)	pound sterling
ein Dollar (*m*)	dollar

ein Zehnmarkschein
a 10 mark note

ich möchte gern 500 Mark in Pfund umtauschen
I'd like to change 500 marks into pounds

was ist der Wechselkurs für das englische Pfund?
what is the exchange rate for the pound?

ich möchte gern mit Kreditkarte bezahlen
I'd like to pay by credit card

akzeptieren Sie Reiseschecks?
do you take traveller's cheques?

ich spare für ein Motorrad
I'm saving up for a motorbike

ich habe 1000 Mark Schulden
I have debts of 1000 marks

ich habe mir 2000 Mark von meinem Vater geliehen
I borrowed 2000 marks from my father

ich bin pleite
I'm broke

mein Konto ist überzogen
I'm overdrawn

ich komme nur schwer mit dem Geld aus
I find it hard to make ends meet

See also Sections **10 WORK** *and* **18 SHOPPING**.

32. AKTUELLE THEMEN
TOPICAL ISSUES

diskutieren	to discuss
sich streiten	to argue
kritisieren	to criticize
verteidigen	to defend
denken	to think
meinen	to think, to be of the opinion
glauben	to believe
für	for, in favour of
gegen	against, opposed to
intolerant	intolerant
tolerant	broad-minded
warum	why
wieso	why, how come
ein Thema (*n*)	topic
ein Problem (*n*)	problem
ein Argument (*n*)	argument
die Gesellschaft	society
ein Vorurteil (*n*)	prejudice
die Moral	morals
die Mentalität	mentality
die Abrüstung	disarmament
die Atomenergie	nuclear energy
die Atombombe	(nuclear) Bomb
der Frieden	peace
der Krieg	war
die Armut	poverty
die Not	destitution
die Arbeitslosigkeit	unemployment
die Gewalt	violence
die Kriminalität	criminality
die Empfängnisverhütung	contraception

die Abtreibung	abortion
die Homosexualität	homosexuality
ein Homosexueller (*m*)	gay man
eine Lesbierin	Lesbian
Aids	Aids
der Sexismus	sexism
ein Chauvinist (*m*)	male chauvinist
ein(e) Fanatiker(in)	fanatic
die Frauenbefreiung	women's liberation
die Frauenbewegung	Women's Liberation Movement
der Feminismus	feminism
die Gleichheit	equality
der Rassismus	racism
ein Schwarzer, eine Schwarze	black person
ein(e) Ausländer(in)	foreigner
ein Einwanderer, eine Einwanderin	immigrant
ein politischer Flüchtling	political refugee
das politische Asyl	political asylum
der Alkohol	alcohol
ein(e) Alkoholiker(in)	alcoholic
Drogen (*pl*)	drugs
eine Überdosis	overdose
die Sucht	addiction
das Haschisch	hashish
das Kokain	cocaine
das Heroin	heroin
der Drogenhandel	drug trafficking
ein Dealer (*m*)	dealer

ich stimme nicht mit dir überein
I don't agree (with you)

sie sind sich einig
they agree

sie ist rauschgiftsüchtig
she's a drug addict

33. POLITIK
POLITICS

regieren	to govern
herrschen	to rule
organisieren	to organize
demonstrieren	to demonstrate
wählen	to elect, to vote
stimmen für/gegen	to vote for/against
unterdrücken	to repress
abschaffen	to abolish, to do away with
auferlegen	to impose
verstaatlichen	to nationalize
entstaatlichen	to privatize
importieren	to import
exportieren	to export
national	national
international	international
politisch	political
demokratisch	democratic
konservativ	conservative
sozialistisch	socialist
sozialdemokratisch	social-democratic
liberal	liberal
kommunistisch	communist
marxistisch	Marxist
faschistisch	fascist
anarchistisch	anarchic
kapitalistisch	capitalist
extremistisch	extremist
radikal	radical
gemäßigt	moderate
links	left wing
rechts	right wing
linksradikal	left-wing radical
rechtsradikal	right-wing radical

eine Nation	nation
ein Land (*n*)	country
ein Staat (*m*)	state
eine Republik	republic
die Bundesrepublik Deutschland (BRD)	Federal Republic of Germany (FRG)
die Deutsche Demokratische Republik (DDR)	German Democratic Republic (GDR)
eine Monarchie	monarchy
die Heimat	homeland
das Ausland	overseas, abroad
die Regierung	government
das Parlament	parliament
das Kabinett	Cabinet
die Verfassung	constitution
das Staatsoberhaupt	Head of State
der Regierungschef	head of government
der Bundeskanzler	German/ Austrian Chancellor
der Bundespräsident	Federal German/Austrian President
der Premierminister, die Premierministerin	Prime Minister
ein(e) Minister(in)	minister
der Außenminister	foreign minister
ein Abgeordneter, eine Abgeordnete	MP
ein(e) Politiker(in)	politician
ein(e) Bürgermeister(in)	mayor(ess)
die Politik	politics
Wahlen (*pl*)	elections
eine Partei	political party
die Rechte	right
die Linke	left
das Wahlrecht	right to vote
ein Wahlkreis (*m*)	constituency
die Wahlurne	ballot box
ein(e) Kandidat(in)	candidate
der Wahlkampf	election campaign

eine Meinungsumfrage	opinion poll
ein(e) Bürger(in)	citizen
Verhandlungen (*pl*)	negotiations
eine Debatte	debate
ein Gesetz (*n*)	law
eine Krise	crisis
eine Demonstration	demonstration
ein Staatsstreich (*m*)	coup
eine Revolution	revolution
Menschenrechte (*pl*)	human rights
eine Diktatur	dictatorship
eine Ideologie	ideology
die Demokratie	democracy
der Sozialismus	socialism
der Kommunismus	communism
der Faschismus	fascism
der Kapitalismus	capitalism
der Pazifismus	pacifism
die Neutralität	neutrality
die Einheit	unity
die Freiheit	freedom
die öffentliche Meinung	public opinion
der Adel	nobility
die Aristokratie	aristocracy
die Oberschicht	upper class
der Mittelstand	middle classes
die Arbeiterklasse	working class
das Volk	the people
ein König (*m*)	king
eine Königin	queen
ein(e) Kaiser(in)	emperor/empress
ein Prinz (*m*)	prince
eine Prinzessin	princess
die UNO	UN
die Vereinten Nationen (*pl*)	United Nations
die EG	EEC
die Europäische Gemeinschaft	European Community
der Gemeinsame Markt	Common Market

34. KOMMUNIKATION
COMMUNICATING

sagen	to say, to tell
sprechen	to talk, to speak
erzählen	to tell (*story*)
plaudern	to chat
wiederholen	to repeat
hinzufügen	to add
erklären	to declare, to state
ankündigen	to announce
ausdrücken	to express
behaupten	to claim
annehmen	to suppose
bezweifeln	to doubt
begreifen	to understand
kapieren	to understand, to catch on
sich unterhalten mit	to speak with
sich streiten	to argue
informieren	to inform
zu verstehen geben	to give to understand
erwähnen	to mention
versprechen	to promise
rufen	to shout
schreien	to yell, to shriek
flüstern	to whisper
murmeln	to murmur, to mumble
stottern	to stammer
sich aufregen	to get worked up
antworten	to reply, to answer
entgegnen	to reply, to retort
recht haben	to be right
unrecht haben	to be wrong
überreden	to persuade
überzeugen	to convince
beeinflussen	to influence

zustimmen	to agree
ablehnen	to decline
widersprechen	to contradict
bestreiten	to contest
einwenden	to object
widerlegen	to refute
übertreiben	to exaggerate
betonen	to emphasize
vorhersagen	to predict
sich entschuldigen	to apologize
vorgeben	to pretend
täuschen	to deceive
schmeicheln	to flatter
kritisieren	to criticize
verleumden	to slander
bestreiten	to deny
zugeben	to admit
überzeugt	convinced
überzeugend	convincing
wahr	true
falsch	false
ein Gespräch (n)	conversation
eine Unterhaltung	talk
eine Diskussion	discussion
ein Streit (m)	argument
ein Dialog (m)	dialogue
ein Monolog (m)	monologue
eine Rede	speech
eine Vorlesung	lecture
eine Debatte	debate
eine Konferenz	conference
eine Erklärung	statement
das Gerede	gossip
ein Gerücht (n)	rumour
die Meinung	opinion
die Ansicht	view
eine Idee	idea

der Standpunkt	point of view
ein Argument (n)	argument
ein Mißverständnis (n)	misunderstanding
die Kritik	criticism
ein Einwand (m)	objection
eine Erklärung	declaration, statement
offen	frankly
allgemein	generally
natürlich	naturally
selbstverständlich	of course
wirklich	really
völlig	entirely
zweifellos	undoubtedly
vielleicht	maybe, perhaps
aber	but
jedoch	however
oder	or
und	and
falls	if
weil	because
deshalb	therefore
also	therefore, so
dank (+gen)	thanks to
trotz (+gen)	despite
außer (+ dat)	except
über	about, on
mit (+ dat)	with
ohne	without
fast	almost

nicht wahr?
isn't it?/ don't you?/ aren't they? *etc*

du magst ihn nicht, oder? – doch
you don't like him, do you? – yes, I do

es ist mir egal
I don't mind

See also Sections **32 TOPICAL ISSUES** *and* **36 PHONE.**

35. BRIEFVERKEHR
LETTER WRITING

schreiben	to write
kritzeln	to scribble
notieren	to jot down
beschreiben	to describe
(auf der Maschine) schreiben	to type
tippen	to type
ausfüllen	to fill out
unterschreiben	to sign
beantworten	to answer
senden	to send
schicken	to send
kleben	to stick
zukleben	to seal
freimachen	to put a stamp on, to frank
frankieren	to frank
wiegen	to weigh
absenden	to post
einwerfen	to post
zurücksenden	to send back
nachsenden	to forward
beilegen	to enclose
enthalten	to contain
erhalten	to receive
antworten	to reply
lesbar	legible, readable
unleserlich	illegible
per Luftpost	by airmail
per Eilboten	by express delivery
per Einschreiben	by registered mail
Anlagen	enclosures
von	from (*person*)
aus	from (*country*)
ein Brief (*m*)	letter

eine Postkarte	postcard
eine Ansichtskarte	picture postcard
die Post	mail
das Schreibpapier	writing paper
ein Zettel (*m*)	note
das Datum	date
die Unterschrift	signature
ein (Brief)umschlag (*m*)	envelope
die Adresse	address
die Anschrift	address
der Empfänger, die Empfängerin	addressee
der Absender, die Absenderin	sender
die Postleitzahl	postcode
der Ort	town
die Straße	street
eine Briefmarke	stamp
das Postwertzeichen	postage stamp
ein Briefkasten (*m*)	postbox
der Schlitz	slot
die Leerung	collection
die Post	post office
das Postamt	post office
der Schalter	counter
das Porto	postage
eine Briefwaage	letter scales
eine Frankiermaschine	franking machine
die Aufbewahrungsstelle	poste restante
ein Paket (*n*)	parcel
ein Päckchen (*n*)	small parcel
ein Telegramm (*n*)	telegram, telemessage
die Empfangsbestätigung	acknowledgement of receipt
ein Formular (*n*)	form
eine Geldanweisung	postal order
der Inhalt	contents
der Briefträger	postman
ein(e) Brieffreund(in)	penfriend
die Handschrift	handwriting
ein Kugelschreiber (*m*)	biro (*R*)

ein Kuli (*m*)	biro (*R*)
ein Bleistift (*m*)	pencil
ein Füller (*m*)	fountain pen
eine Schreibmaschine	typewriter
ein Textverarbeitungsgerät (*n*)	wordprocessor
eine Notiz	note
der Text	text
die Seite	page
ein Paragraph (*m*)	paragraph
ein Absatz (*m*)	paragraph
eine Linie	line
ein Wort (*n*)	word
der Stil	style
die Fortsetzung	continuation
ein Zitat (*n*)	quotation
der Titel	title
der Rand	margin
die Anlage	enclosure
eine Geburtstagskarte	birthday card
eine Weihnachtskarte	Christmas card
ein Liebesbrief (*m*)	love letter
eine Beschwerde	complaint

Sehr geehrte Herren/Damen und Herren
Dear Sirs/Sir or Madam

Lieber Wolfgang/Liebe Inge
Dear Wolfgang/Inge

mit freundlichen Grüßen
Yours (faithfully/sincerely)

hochachtungsvoll
Yours faithfully

herzliche Grüße
(lots of) love

ich hätte gern drei Briefmarken zu 18 Pence
I'd like three 18 pence stamps

36. TELEFON
THE PHONE

anrufen	to call, to phone
wählen	to dial
auflegen	to hang up
zurückrufen	to call back
sich melden	to answer
telefonieren	to phone, to ring, to make a phone call
sich verwählen	to dial a wrong number
den Hörer abnehmen	to lift the receiver
das Telefon	phone
der Fernsprecher	telephone
ein Tastentelefon (*n*)	push-button phone
die Taste	button, key
der Hörer	receiver, earpiece
das Amtszeichen	dialling tone
der (Geld)einwurf	slot
die Wählscheibe	dial
das Telefonbuch	phone book
die gelben Seiten	yellow pages
eine Telefonzelle	phone box
ein Ferngespräch (*n*)	long distance call
ein Ortsgespräch (*n*)	local call
ein R-Gespräch (*n*)	reverse charge call
die Vorwahl	dialling code
die Rufnummer	number
eine falsche Nummer	wrong number
die Auskunft	enquiries
die Vermittlung	operator
die Zeitansage	speaking clock
der Notruf	emergency
ein drahtloses Telefon	cordless phone
ein Autotelefon (*n*)	carphone
besetzt	engaged

außer Betrieb　　　　　　　　　　out of order

er hat seine Mutter angerufen
he phoned his mother

das Telefon klingelt/schellt
the phone's ringing

wer spricht bitte?
who's speaking?

hallo, hier (ist) Karl-Heinz
hello, this is Karl-Heinz

ich möchte gern mit Martin/Melanie sprechen
I'd like to speak to Martin/Melanie

am Apparat
speaking

bleiben Sie am Apparat
hang on

es ist besetzt
it's engaged

tut mir leid, er ist nicht da
I'm sorry, he's not in

möchten Sie eine Nachricht hinterlassen?
would you like to leave a message?

wer spricht bitte?
who shall I say called? who's calling?

entschuldigen Sie, ich habe mich verwählt
sorry, I've got the wrong number

meine Nummer ist zweiundzwanzig, einundvierzig, null zwo
my number is two two four one zero two

ich muß jetzt Schluß machen
I'll have to go now

auf Wiederhören
goodbye

37. GRUSS- UND HÖFLICHKEITSFORMEN GREETINGS AND POLITE PHRASES

grüßen	to greet
begrüßen	to welcome
vorstellen	to introduce
ausdrücken	to express
danken (+*dat*)	to thank
gratulieren	to congratulate
wünschen	to wish
sich verabschieden	to say goodbye
sich entschuldigen	to apologize
ein Kompliment (*n*)	compliment
guten Tag!	hello, good morning/afternoon
guten Morgen!	good morning
guten Abend!	good evening
hallo!	hi
grüß Gott!	hello, goodbye
tschüs!	cheerio
auf Wiedersehen!	goodbye, cheerio
gute Nacht!	good night, sleep well
freut mich!	pleased to meet you
wie geht es dir/Ihnen?	how are you?
wie geht's?	how are things?
bis bald!	see you soon
bis gleich!	see you soon
bis später!	see you later
bis nachher!	see you later
bis morgen!	see you tomorrow
guten Appetit!	enjoy your meal!
viel Glück!	good luck!
viel Spaß/Vergnügen!	have fun
alles Gute!	all the best

gute Reise/Fahrt!	have a good trip, safe journey
gute Heimfahrt!	safe journey home
willkommen	welcome
Entschuldigung!	sorry!
Verzeihung!	sorry!
(wie) bitte?	sorry? (*didn't hear*), pardon?
tut mir leid	I'm sorry
ja	yes
nein	no
nein danke	no thanks
ja bitte	yes please
mit Vergnügen	with pleasure
bitte	please
bitte (schön/sehr)	you're welcome, here you are
danke (schön/sehr)	thank you
vielen Dank	thank you very much
keine Ursache	not at all
gern geschehen	you're welcome
auf dein/Ihr Wohl	good health!
zum Wohl!	cheers!
prost!	cheers!
Gesundheit!	bless you (*after sneezing*)
in Ordnung	OK
okay	OK
um so besser	so much the better
macht nichts	never mind

Festlichkeiten   festivities

fröhliche Weihnachten!	merry Christmas!
frohes neues Jahr!	happy New Year!
viele Grüße!	best wishes!
frohe Ostern!	happy Easter!
viel Glück zum Geburtstag!	happy birthday!
herzlichen Glückwunsch!	congratulations!
bravo!	well done!

darf ich Ihnen Gerd Müller vorstellen?
may I introduce Gerd Müller?

ich möchte Ihnen mein Beileid aussprechen
please accept my sympathy

bitte nehmen Sie Platz!
please take a seat

das macht mir nichts aus
I don't mind

es geht
it's all right

das kommt darauf an
it depends

viel Glück! – danke gleichfalls!
good luck! – thanks, same to you

ich bin Ihnen sehr dankbar
I'm very grateful to you

nichts zu danken
don't mention it

das tut mir sehr leid
I'm terribly sorry

tut mir leid, Sie zu stören
I'm sorry to bother you

stört es Sie, wenn ich rauche?
do you mind if I smoke?

können Sie mir Ihren Kugelschreiber leihen? – bitte
can you lend me your ballpoint? – here you are

entschuldigen Sie, können Sie mir sagen ...?
excuse me please, could you tell me ...?

wie schade
what a pity

38. REISEVORBEREITUNG UND ZOLLABFERTIGUNG
PLANNING A HOLIDAY AND CUSTOMS FORMALITIES

in Urlaub fahren	to go on holiday
buchen	to book
mieten	to rent
bestätigen	to confirm
rückgängig machen	to cancel
sich informieren (über)	to get information (about)
sich erkundigen (nach)	to enquire (about)
packen	to pack
einpacken	to pack
die Koffer packen	to pack one's suitcases
mitnehmen	to take
vergessen	to forget
eine Versicherung abschließen	to take out insurance
seinen Reisepaß verlängern lassen	to renew one's passport
sich impfen lassen	to be vaccinated
durchsuchen	to search
auspacken	to unpack
verzollen	to declare
schmuggeln	to smuggle
kontrollieren	to check
der Urlaub	holidays
die Ferien (*pl*)	holidays
ein Ausflug (*m*)	outing
eine Rundfahrt	tour
die Saison	season
ein Reisebüro (*n*)	travel agent's
eine Touristen-Informationsstelle	tourist information centre
ein Prospekt (*m*)	leaflet, brochure

eine Broschüre	leaflet, brochure
eine Pauschalreise	package tour
ein Reiseführer (*m*)	guide(book)
der Reiseleiter	courier
die Reservierung	booking, reservation
eine Anzahlung	deposit
eine Liste	list
das Gepäck	luggage
ein Koffer (*m*)	suitcase
eine Reisetasche	travel bag
ein Rucksack (*m*)	rucksack
ein Etikett (*n*)	label
ein Kulturbeutel (*m*)	toilet bag
der (Reise)paß	passport
der Personalausweis	identity card
die grüne Karte	green card (*insurance*)
das Visum	visa
die Fahrkarte	ticket
ein Reisescheck (*m*)	traveller's cheque
eine Reiseversicherung	travel insurance
der Zoll	customs
der Zollbeamte	customs officer
die Grenze	border
die Paßkontrolle	passport control
die Zollkontrolle	customs
zollfrei	duty-free

nichts zu verzollen
nothing to declare

ich freue mich auf meinen Urlaub
I'm looking forward to going on holiday

See also Sections **39** *to* **41 RAILWAYS, FLYING** *and* **PUBLIC TRANSPORT** *and* **42 HOTEL**.

39. EISENBAHN
RAILWAYS

eine Fahrkarte lösen	to buy a ticket
reservieren	to reserve, to book
umsteigen	to change
einsteigen	to get on/in
aussteigen	to get off
Verspätung haben	to be late
pünktlich	on time
planmäßig	on schedule
verspätet	late
reserviert	reserved
besetzt	taken, engaged
frei	free
Raucher	smoking
Nichtraucher	non-smoking

der Bahnhof — the station

der Bahnhof	station
die (Deutsche) Bundesbahn	German Railways
die Eisenbahn	railways
der Fahrkartenschalter	ticket office
der Fahrkartenautomat	ticket vending machine
die Auskunft	information
die Reiseauskunft	travel information
die Anzeigetafel	indicator board
der Wartesaal	waiting room
der Bahnhofsimbiß	station buffet
die Erfrischungen	refreshments
das Gepäck	luggage
die Gepäckannahme	left luggage
die Gepäckaufbewahrung	left luggage
die Gepäckausgabe	left luggage collection
die Gepäckrückgabe	left luggage collection

Schließfächer (*n*)	left luggage lockers
ein Kofferkuli (*m*)	luggage trolley
der Bahnhofsvorsteher	station supervisor
der Schaffner	guard, ticket collector
ein Eisenbahner (*m*)	railwayman
ein Gepäckträger (*m*)	porter
ein Reisender, eine Reisende	passenger

der Zug   the train

ein Zug (*m*)	train
ein Güterzug (*m*)	freight train
ein durchgehender Zug	through train
ein Nahverkehrszug (*m*)	local train
ein Eilzug (*m*)	fast train
ein Schnellzug (*m*)	express train
ein Intercity-Zug (*m*)	Intercity train
ein Autoreisezug (*m*)	motorail train
ein Dieseltriebwagen (*m*)	diesel train
ein D-Zug (*m*)	express train
ein TEE (*m*)	Trans-Europe-Express train
die Lok(omotive)	locomotive, engine
eine Dampflok	steam engine
der Speisewagen	dining car
ein Wagen (*m*)	coach
ein Waggon (*m*)	coach, carriage
ein Liegewagen (*m*)	couchette carriage
ein Schlafwagen (*m*)	sleeper
der Gepäckwagen	luggage van
das Abteil	compartment
ein Schlafplatz (*m*)	sleeping berth, couchette
die Toilette	toilet
die Tür	door
das Fenster	window
der Sitz(platz)	seat
die Gepäckablage	luggage rack
das Gepäcknetz	luggage rack
die Notbremse	emergency brake, communication cord

das Alarmsignal	alarm

die Reise — the journey

der Bahnsteig	platform
das Gleis	platform; track
Geleise (*pl*)	tracks
die Bahnlinie	line
das Streckennetz	network
ein Bahnübergang (*m*)	level crossing
ein Tunnel (*m*)	tunnel
eine Haltestelle	stop
die Ankunft	arrival
die Abfahrt	departure
die Verbindung	connection

Fahrkarten — tickets

die Fahrkarte	ticket
der Fahrausweis	ticket
der Fahrschein	ticket
der ermäßigte Fahrpreis	reduced rate
ein Erwachsener, eine Erwachsene	adult
ein Kind (*n*)	child
eine Einzelfahrkarte	single (ticket)
eine Rückfahrkarte	return (ticket)
die Klasse	class
die erste Klasse	first class
die zweite Klasse	second class
eine Reservierung	reservation
der Fahrplan	timetable
Sonn- und Feiertage	Sundays and public holidays
Wochentage (*pl*)	weekdays
werktags	on weekdays (and Saturdays)
sonntags	on Sundays

per Bahn
by rail

ich bin mit dem Zug nach München gefahren
I went to Munich by train

eine einfache Fahrkarte/eine Rückfahrkarte nach Köln, bitte
a single/return to Cologne, please

einmal Köln hin und zurück, bitte
one return to Cologne, please

wann fährt der nächste/letzte Zug nach Mannheim?
when is the next/last train to Mannheim?

der Zug aus Hamburg hat zwanzig Minuten Verspätung
the train arriving from Hamburg is 20 minutes late

wir haben in Frankfurt 50 Minuten Aufenthalt
we have a 50 minute wait in Frankfurt

Sie müssen in Düsseldorf umsteigen
you have to change at Düsseldorf

der Zug fährt über Essen
the train goes via Essen

ist dieser Platz besetzt?
is this seat taken?

"nicht hinauslehnen"
'do not lean out'

"die Fahrkarten bitte"
'tickets please'

"noch jemand zugestiegen?"
'any more tickets please?'

er ist (mit dem) Intercity nach Berlin gefahren
he went to Berlin on the Intercity

er hat mich vom Bahnhof abgeholt
he came and picked me up at the station

gute Reise!
have a good journey!

40. FLIEGEN
FLYING

abfliegen	to leave
abheben	to take off
landen	to land
fliegen	to fly
einchecken	to check in

am Flughafen — at the airport

der Flughafen	airport
die Start- und Landebahn	runway
die Runway	runway
der Kontrollturm	control tower
die Fluggesellschaft	airline
die Auskunft	information
die Abfertigung	check-in
das Handgepäck	hand luggage
der Duty-free-Laden	duty-free shop
die Abflughalle	departure lounge
die Paßkontrolle	passport control
die Bordkarte	boarding pass
der Flugsteig	gate
die Gepäckausgabe	baggage claim
der Terminal	terminal

an Bord — on board

ein Flugzeug (*n*)	plane
eine Maschine	plane
ein Überschallflugzeug (*n*)	supersonic plane
ein Düsenflugzeug (*n*)	jet
ein Jumbo-Jet (*m*)	jumbo jet
ein Charterflugzeug (*n*)	charter plane
ein Hubschrauber (*m*)	helicopter

der Flügel	wing
der Propeller	propeller
der Sicherheitsgurt	seat belt
der Notausstieg	emergency exit
ein Fenster (*n*)	window
ein Sitz (*m*)	seat
der Flug	flight
ein Direktflug (*m*)	direct flight
ein Inlandsflug (*m*)	domestic flight
ein Auslandsflug (*m*)	international flight
die Höhe	altitude
die Geschwindigkeit	speed
der Abflug	departure
der Start	take-off
die Ankunft	arrival
die Landung	landing
eine Notlandung	emergency landing
eine Zwischenlandung	stop-over
eine Verzögerung	delay
die Besatzung	crew
der Pilot	pilot
eine Stewardeß	stewardess
ein Steward (*m*)	steward
ein Passagier (*m*)	passenger (*male and female*)
der Luftpirat	hijacker
startbereit	ready for take-off
gestrichen	cancelled
verzögert	delayed
Raucher	smoking
Nichtraucher	non-smoking

ich möchte gern einen Nichtraucherplatz
I'd like a no smoking seat

Passagiere des Fluges BA209 bitte zum Flugsteig 17
flight BA209 now boarding at gate number 17

bitte anschnallen
fasten your seat belt

41. ÖFFENTLICHER NAHVERKEHR
PUBLIC TRANSPORT

einsteigen	to get on
aussteigen	to get off
warten (auf +*acc*)	to wait (for)
abfahren	to leave
ankommen	to arrive
umsteigen	to change
anhalten	to stop
sich beeilen	to hurry
verpassen	to miss
seinen Fahrschein entwerten	to put one's ticket in the ticket-stamping machine
schwarzfahren	to dodge paying the fare
ein Bus (*m*)	bus
ein Autobus (*m*)	bus
ein (Reise)bus (*m*)	coach
die Straßenbahn	tram
die U-Bahn	underground
die S-Bahn	local train
ein Nahverkehrszug (*m*)	local train
ein Taxi (*n*)	taxi
der Fahrer	driver
der Schaffner	inspector, conductor
ein Passagier (*m*)	passenger (*male and female*)
ein Fahrgast (*m*)	passenger (*male and female*)
ein(e) Schwarzfahrer(in)	fare dodger
der Busbahnhof	bus station
der Bahnhof	station
ein Wartehäuschen (*n*)	bus shelter
eine Bushaltestelle	bus stop
eine Straßenbahnhaltestelle	tram stop
der Fahrkartenschalter	booking office
ein Fahrkartenautomat (*m*)	ticket machine
der Ausgang	exit

die Linie	line
der Einstieg	entrance
der Ausstieg	exit
die Abfahrt	departure
die Richtung	direction
die Ankunft	arrival
die Spitze	front
das Ende	back
der Sitz(platz)	seat
eine Fahrkarte	ticket
ein Fahrschein (*m*)	ticket
der Fahrpreis	fare
eine Mehrfahrtenkarte	strip of tickets
ein Fahrscheinheft (*n*)	book of tickets
eine Tageskarte	day ticket
eine Zeitkarte	season ticket
eine Wochenkarte	weekly ticket
eine Monatskarte	monthly ticket
eine Netzkarte	runabout ticket
ein Erwachsener, eine Erwachsene	adult
ein Kind (*n*)	child
der Tarif	fares
der Spartarif	economy fare
die Ermäßigung	reduction
ein Zuschlag (*m*)	excess fare
der Nachtzuschlag	night-time supplement
die Stoßzeit	rush hour

ich fahre mit dem Bus zur Schule
I go to school by bus

mit welchem Bus kann ich zum Dom fahren?
what bus can I get to go to the Cathedral?

wo ist die nächste U-Bahn-Station?
where is the nearest underground station?

ist dieser Fahrschein noch gültig?
is this ticket still valid?

See also Section **39 RAILWAYS**.

42. IM HOTEL
AT THE HOTEL

(voll) belegt	no vacancies
Zimmer frei	vacancies
geschlossen	closed
komfortabel	comfortable
inbegriffen	included
ein Hotel (*n*)	hotel
eine Pension	guest house
Fremdenzimmer (*pl*)	rooms to let
die Vollpension	full board
die Halbpension	half board
der Preis pro Nacht	price per day
die Rechnung	bill
die Mehrwertsteuer	VAT
das Trinkgeld	tip
die Bedienung	service
der Empfang	reception
eine Beschwerde	complaint
eine Reklamation	complaint
eine Reservierung	reservation
das Restaurant	restaurant
der Speiseraum	dining room
die Bar	bar
ein Parkplatz (*m*)	car park
ein Aufzug (*m*)	lift
das Frühstück	breakfast
das Mittagessen	lunch
das Abendessen	dinner
ein Gast (*m*)	guest (*male and female*)
der Direktor	manager
der Empfangschef	receptionist (*male*)
die Empfangsdame	receptionist (*female*)
der Portier	porter

der Nachtportier	night porter
das Zimmermädchen	chambermaid
der Zimmerservice	room service

das Zimmer   the room

ein Zimmer (*n*)	room
ein Einzelzimmer (*n*)	single room
ein Doppelzimmer (*n*)	double room
ein Zweibettzimmer (*n*)	twin room
ein Doppelbett (*n*)	double bed
ein Bett (*n*)	bed
ein Kinderbett (*n*)	cot
ein Badezimmer (*n*)	bathroom
ein Bad (*n*)	bath
eine Dusche	shower
ein Waschbecken (*n*)	washbasin
das warme Wasser	hot water
die Toilette	toilet
die Klimaanlage	air conditioning
der Notausgang	emergency exit
ein Balkon (*m*)	balcony
die Aussicht	view
der Schlüssel	key

Übernachtung mit Frühstück
bed and breakfast

ein Zwei-/Drei-Sterne-Hotel
a two/three star hotel

haben Sie Zimmer frei?
have you got any vacancies?

im zweiten Stock
on the second floor

ein Zimmer mit Blick auf die Berge
a room with a view of the mountains

das Hotel hat eine herrliche Lage
the hotel is beautifully situated

ein Zimmer mit eigenem Bad
a room with a private bathroom

ich möchte gern ein Einzelzimmer/ein Doppelzimmer
I'd like a single/double room

für wieviel Nächte?
for how many nights?

wir sind voll belegt
we're full

könnten Sie mich bitte um sieben Uhr wecken?
could you please call me at seven a.m.?

ich habe Zimmer Nummer sieben
my room number is 7

können Sie meine Rechnung fertigmachen, bitte?
could you make up my bill please?

"nicht stören"
'do not disturb'

43. CAMPING, WOHNWAGEN UND JUGENDHERBERGEN
CAMPING, CARAVANNING AND YOUTH HOSTELS

campen	to camp
zelten	to camp
Camping machen	to go camping
wild zelten	to camp in the wild
Ferien im Wohnwagen machen	to go caravanning
per Anhalter fahren	to hitch-hike
trampen	to hitch-hike
das Zelt aufbauen	to pitch the tent
das Zelt abbauen	to take down the tent
im Freien übernachten	to sleep out in the open
das Camping	camping
ein Campingplatz (m)	campsite
ein(e) Camper(in)	camper
ein Zelt (n)	tent
eine Luftmatratze	Lilo (R)
das Überzelt	fly sheet
eine Bodenplane	ground sheet
ein Zeltpflock (m)	peg
ein Hering (m)	peg
ein Seil (n)	rope
ein Feuer (n)	fire
ein Lagerfeuer (n)	campfire
das Campinggaz (R)	Calorgas (R)
eine Nachfüllflasche	refill
ein Ofen (m)	stove
das Kochgeschirr	billy can
ein Taschenmesser (n)	pocket knife, penknife
ein Eimer (m)	bucket
ein klappbarer Tisch	foldaway table
ein Klapptisch (m)	foldaway table
ein Klappstuhl (m)	foldaway chair

ein Schlafsack (*m*)	sleeping bag
eine Taschenlampe	torch
die sanitären Anlagen	showers and toilets
die Duschen (*pl*)	showers
die Toiletten (*pl*)	toilets
das Trinkwasser	drinking water
der Abfall	rubbish
ein Abfalleimer (*m*)	rubbish bin
eine Stechmücke	midge, gnat
der Wohnwagenurlaub	caravanning
ein Wohnwagenplatz (*m*)	caravan site
ein Wohnwagen (*m*)	caravan
ein Campingbus (*m*)	Dormobile (*R*)
ein Anhänger (*m*)	trailer
eine Jugendherberge	youth hostel
der Herbergsvater	youth hostel warden
die Herbergsmutter	youth hostel warden
der Schlafraum	dormitory
der Waschraum	washroom
der Mitgliedsausweis	membership card
ein Rucksack (*m*)	rucksack
das Trampen	hitch-hiking

dürfen wir hier zelten?
may we camp here?

"Zelten verboten"
'no camping'

"Trinkwasser"
'drinking water'

44. AM MEER
AT THE SEASIDE

schwimmen	to swim
treiben	to float, to drift
planschen	to splash about
tauchen	to dive
ertrinken	to drown
sich bräunen	to get a tan
baden	to bathe
sonnenbaden	to sunbathe
einen Sonnenbrand bekommen	to get sunburnt
sich schälen	to peel
seekrank sein	to be seasick
segeln	to go sailing, to sail
surfen	to surf
windsurfen	to windsurf
rudern	to row
sinken	to sink
kentern	to capsize
schattig	shady
sonnig	sunny
sonnengebräunt	tanned
im Schatten	in the shade
in der Sonne	in the sun
an Bord	on board
vor (der Küste von)	off the coast of
das Meer	sea
die See	sea
ein See (m)	lake
der Strand	beach
der Sand	sand
die Kieselsteine (pl)	shingle
ein Fels(en) (m)	rock
eine Klippe	cliff

eine Welle	wave
die Flut	(high) tide
die Ebbe	low tide
die Strömung	current
die Küste	coast
ein Hafen (m)	harbour
der Kai	quay
die Strandpromenade	esplanade
ein Leuchtturm (m)	lighthouse
eine Boje	buoy
der Horizont	horizon
die Überfahrt	crossing
ein Rettungsschwimmer (m)	lifeguard
ein(e) Schwimmlehrer(in)	swimming instructor
ein(e) Schwimmer(in)	bather, swimmer
eine Muschel	shell
ein Fisch (m)	fish
eine Möwe	seagull
eine Qualle	jellyfish

Schiffe und Boote   boats

ein Schiff (n)	ship
ein Boot (n)	boat
ein Ruderboot (n)	rowing boat
ein Segelboot (n)	sailing boat
ein Motorboot (n)	motor boat
ein Segelschiff (n)	sailing ship
eine Jacht	yacht
ein Dampfer (m)	steamer
eine Fähre	ferry
eine Autofähre	car ferry
ein Dingi (n)	dinghy
ein Gummiboot (n)	rubber dinghy
ein Tretboot (n)	pedalo
ein Ruder (n)	oar
das Segel	sail
ein Anker (m)	anchor

Strandzubehör   things for the beach

ein Badeanzug (*m*)	swimsuit
eine Badehose	trunks
ein Bikini (*m*)	bikini
eine Badekappe	bathing cap
eine Taucherbrille	goggles
ein Schnorchel (*m*)	snorkel
Schwimmflossen (*pl*)	flippers
ein Rettungsring (*m*)	lifebelt
eine Luftmatratze	air mattress, Lilo (*R*)
ein Liegestuhl (*m*)	deckchair
ein Badetuch (*n*)	towel
ein Sonnenschirm (*m*)	parasol
eine Sonnenbrille	sunglasses
das Sonnenöl	suntan oil/lotion
ein Sonnenbrand (*m*)	sunburn
ein Sonnenstich (*m*)	sunstroke
ein Spaten (*m*)	spade
eine Harke	rake
ein Eimer (*m*)	bucket
eine Sandburg	sand castle
eine Frisbee-Scheibe	frisbee
ein Ball (*m*)	ball

ich kann nicht schwimmen
I can't swim

"Baden verboten"
'no bathing'

"Mann über Bord!"
'man overboard!'

45. GEOGRAPHIE
GEOGRAPHICAL TERMS

der Kontinent	continent
der Erdteil	continent
ein Land (*n*)	country
ein Staat (*m*)	state
ein Entwicklungsland (*n*)	developing country
ein Gebiet (*n*)	area, region
ein Bundesland (*n*)	'Land' (or state) of the Federal Republic of Germany
der Bezirk	district
eine Stadt	town, city
ein Dorf (*n*)	village
die Hauptstadt	capital city
ein Gebirge (*n*)	mountains
ein Berg (*m*)	mountain, hill
eine Bergkette	mountain chain
ein Hügel (*m*)	hill
eine Klippe	cliff
der Gipfel	summit
die Spitze	peak
der Paß	pass
die Schlucht	ravine
ein Tal (*n*)	valley
eine Ebene	plain
ein Plateau (*n*)	plateau
ein Gletscher (*m*)	glacier
ein Vulkan (*m*)	volcano
das Meer	sea
die See	sea
der Ozean	ocean
der See	lake
der Fluß	river
der Strom	(large) river

der Bach	stream
der Kanal	canal
der Teich	pond
die Quelle	spring
die Küste	coast
eine Insel	island
eine Halbinsel	peninsula
das Kap	promontory
die Bucht	bay
die Mündung	estuary
die Wüste	desert
der Wald	forest
die Heide	heath
die Breite	latitude
die Länge	longitude
die Höhe	altitude
die Tiefe	depth
die Fläche	area
die Bevölkerung	population
die Welt	world
das Universum	universe
die Tropen (*pl*)	Tropics
der Nordpol	North Pole
der Südpol	South Pole
der Äquator	Equator
ein Planet (*m*)	planet
die Erde	earth
die Sonne	sun
der Mond	moon
ein Stern (*m*)	star

welches ist der höchste Berg Europas?
what is the highest mountain in Europe?

See also Sections **46 COUNTRIES** *and* **47 NATIONALITIES**.

46. LÄNDER, ERDTEILE UND ORTSNAMEN
COUNTRIES, CONTINENTS AND PLACE NAMES

die Landkarte	map

Länder | countries

Ägypten	Egypt
Belgien	Belgium
die Bundesrepublik Deutschland (BRD)	West Germany, Federal Republic of Germany, FRG
China	China
Dänemark	Denmark
die Deutsche Demokratische Republik (DDR)	East Germany, German Democratic Republic, GDR
Deutschland	Germany
England	England
Finnland	Finland
Frankreich	France
Griechenland	Greece
Großbritannien	Great Britain
Holland	Holland
Indien	India
Irland	Ireland, Eire
Israel	Israel
Italien	Italy
Japan	Japan
Kanada	Canada
Libyen	Libya
Luxemburg	Luxembourg
Marokko	Morocco
die Niederlande	Netherlands
Nordirland	Northern Ireland

Norwegen	Norway
Österreich	Austria
Polen	Poland
Portugal	Portugal
Rußland	Russia
Schottland	Scotland
Schweden	Sweden
die Schweiz	Switzerland
die Sowjetunion	Soviet Union
Spanien	Spain
Südafrika	South Africa
die Tschechoslowakei	Czechoslovakia
die Türkei	Turkey
die USA	United States
die UdSSR	USSR
Ungarn	Hungary
die Vereinigten Staaten	USA
das Vereinigte Königreich	United Kingdom
Wales	Wales

Erdteile   continents

Afrika	Africa
Amerika	America
Asien	Asia
Australien	Australia
Europa	Europe
Nordamerika	North America
Südamerika	South America

Städte   cities

Athen	Athens
Brüssel	Brussels
Genf	Geneva
Köln	Cologne
London	London
Moskau	Moscow
München	Munich

Prag	Prague
Rom	Rome
Tokio	Tokyo
Venedig	Venice
Warschau	Warsaw
Wien	Vienna

Gebiete — regions

die Dritte Welt	Third World
der Ostblock	Eastern Bloc countries
der Orient	East
der Nahe Osten	Middle East
der Ferne Osten	Far East
Skandinavien	Scandinavia
Norddeutschland	North Germany
Süddeutschland	South Germany
Bayern	Bavaria
das Rheinland	Rhineland
das schottische Hochland	Scottish Highlands

Meere, Flüsse, Inseln und Gebirge — seas, rivers, islands and mountains

das Mittelmeer	Mediterranean
die Nordsee	North Sea
die Ostsee	Baltic
der Atlantik	Atlantic
der Pazifik	Pacific
der Indische Ozean	Indian Ocean
der Kanal	English Channel
der Rhein	Rhine
die Donau	Danube
die Mosel	Moselle
die Themse	Thames
der Bodensee	Lake Constance
die Hebriden	Hebrides
die Antillen (*pl*)	West Indies

Korsika	Corsica
Sardinien	Sardinia
Sizilien	Sicily
der Balkan	Balkans
die Iberische Halbinsel	Iberian Peninsula
der Peloponnes	Peloponnese
Kreta	Crete
Mallorca	Majorca
die Kanalinseln (*pl*)	Channel Islands
die Nordfriesischen Inseln	North Friesian Islands
die Ostfriesischen Inseln	East Friesian Islands
die Alpen (*pl*)	Alps
die Pyrenäen (*pl*)	Pyrenees

ich komme aus England/aus der Türkei
I come from England/Turkey

**ich habe meinen Urlaub in Spanien/in der Schweiz
verbracht**
I spent my holidays in Spain/Switzerland

in Schottland regnet es viel
it rains a lot in Scotland

ich würde gern nach China fahren
I would like to go to China

ich wohne in Berlin
I live in Berlin

ich fahre nach Wien
I'm going to Vienna

See also Section **47 NATIONALITIES**.

47. NATIONALITÄTEN
NATIONALITIES

ausländisch	foreign
fremd	foreign
ein(e) Ägypter(in)	Egyptian
ein(e) Amerikaner(in)	American
ein(e) Australier(in)	Australian
ein(e) Belgier(in)	Belgian
ein Brite, eine Britin	Briton
ein Chinese, eine Chinesin	Chinese
ein Däne, eine Dänin	Dane
ein Deutscher, eine Deutsche	German
ein(e) Engländer(in)	Englishman/woman
ein Finne, eine Finnin	Finn
ein Franzose, eine Französin	Frenchman/woman
ein(e) Holländer(in)	Dutchman/woman
ein(e) Inder(in)	Indian
ein Ire, eine Irin	Irishman/woman
ein Israeli (*m*)	Israeli
ein(e) Italiener(in)	Italian
ein(e) Japaner(in)	Japanese
ein(e) Kanadier(in)	Canadian
ein(e) Libyer(in)	Libyan
ein(e) Luxemburger(in)	man/woman from Luxembourg
ein(e) Marokkaner(in)	Moroccan
ein(e) Niederländer(in)	man/woman from the Netherlands
ein(e) Norweger(in)	Norwegian
ein(e) Österreicher(in)	Austrian
ein Pole, eine Polin	Pole
ein Portugiese, eine Portugiesin	Portuguese
ein Russe, eine Russin	Russian

ein Schotte, eine Schottin	Scot
ein Schwede, eine Schwedin	Swede
ein(e) Schweizer(in)	Swiss
ein(e) Spanier(in)	Spaniard
ein(e) Südafrikaner(in)	South African
ein Tschechoslowake, eine Tschechoslowakin	Czech
ein Türke, eine Türkin	Turk
ein(e) Ungar(in)	Hungarian
ein(e) Waliser(in)	Welshman, Welsh woman
ägyptisch	Egyptian
amerikanisch	American
australisch	Australian
belgisch	Belgian
britisch	British
chinesisch	Chinese
dänisch	Danish
deutsch	German
englisch	English
finnisch	Finnish
französisch	French
holländisch	Dutch
indisch	Indian
irisch	Irish
israelisch	Israeli
italienisch	Italian
japanisch	Japanese
kanadisch	Canadian
libysch	Libyan
luxemburgisch	Luxembourg
marokkanisch	Moroccan
niederländisch	from the Netherlands
nordirisch	Northern Irish
norwegisch	Norwegian
österreichisch	Austrian
polnisch	Polish
portugiesisch	Portuguese
russisch	Russian
schottisch	Scottish
schwedisch	Swedish

schweizerisch	Swiss
sowjetisch	Soviet
spanisch	Spanish
südafrikanisch	South African
tschechoslowakisch	Czech
türkisch	Turkish
ungarisch	Hungarian
walisisch	Welsh
orientalisch	Oriental
fernöstlich	Far Eastern
westlich	Western
östlich	Eastern
afrikanisch	African
asiatisch	Asian
europäisch	European
arabisch	Arabic
skandinavisch	Scandinavian
norddeutsch	North German
süddeutsch	South German
bayrisch	Bavarian
rheinisch	Rhineland
Berliner	from Berlin
Münchner	from Munich
Londoner	from London

Donald ist Schotte
Donald is Scottish

Donald hat schottische Eltern
Donald has Scottish parents

eine Londoner Zeitung
a London newspaper

im In- und Ausland
at home and abroad

48. SPRACHEN
LANGUAGES

lernen	to learn
auswendig lernen	to learn by heart
verstehen	to understand
schreiben	to write
lesen	to read
sprechen	to speak
wiederholen	to repeat
aussprechen	to pronounce
übersetzen	to translate
(sich) verbessern	to improve
meinen	to mean
Deutsch	German
Englisch	English
Französisch	French
Spanisch	Spanish
Portugiesisch	Portuguese
Italienisch	Italian
Griechisch	Greek
Altgriechisch	classical Greek
Lateinisch	Latin
Russisch	Russian
Chinesisch	Chinese
Japanisch	Japanese
Gälisch	Gaelic
eine Sprache	language
die Muttersprache	native language
eine Fremdsprache	foreign language
neuere Sprachen (*pl*)	modern languages
tote Sprachen (*pl*)	dead languages
der Wortschatz	vocabulary
das Vokabular	vocabulary
die Grammatik	grammar
ein Akzent (*m*)	accent

ich verstehe dich/Sie nicht
I don't understand

ich lerne gerade Deutsch
I am learning German

auf deutsch
in German

einen Satz ins Englische übersetzen
to translate a sentence into English

sie spricht fließend Spanisch
she speaks fluent Spanish

Englisch ist seine Muttersprache
English is his native language

was bedeutet das?
what does that mean?

könnten Sie bitte etwas langsamer sprechen?
could you speak more slowly, please?

könnten Sie das bitte noch einmal wiederholen?
could you repeat that, please?

Petra hat ein Talent für Sprachen
Petra is good at languages

er hat Sprachgefühl
he has a feeling for languages

See also Section **47 NATIONALITIES**.

49. FERIEN IN DEUTSCHLAND
HOLIDAYS IN GERMANY

besuchen	to visit
reisen	to travel
sich interessieren für	to be interested in
sich beschweren	to complain
berühmt	famous
malerisch	picturesque
im Urlaub	on holiday

Tourismus — tourism

der Urlaub	holidays
die Ferien (*pl*)	holidays
ein(e) Tourist(in)	tourist
ein(e) Ausländer(in)	foreigner
die Touristen-Informationsstelle	tourist office
das Fremdenverkehrsbüro	tourist information bureau
Sehenswürdigkeiten (*pl*)	sights
ein Urlaubsort (*m*)	resort
Besonderheiten (*pl*)	specialities
ein Souvenir (*n*)	souvenir
ein Andenken (*n*)	souvenir
ein(e) Führer(in)	guide
ein Reiseführer (*m*)	guidebook
ein Sprachführer (*m*)	phrasebook
eine Karte	map
ein Besuch (*m*)	visit
eine Führung	guided tour
eine Fahrt	journey, trip
eine Pauschalreise	package holiday
ein Austausch (*m*)	exchange
der Aufenthalt	stay
ein Ausflug (*m*)	excursion

ein Spaziergang	walk
eine Busreise	coach trip
die Gruppe	group, party
das Konsulat	consulate
die Botschaft	embassy

Deutschland   Germany

die Nationalflagge	national flag
der Bundesadler	German eagle
die Nationalhymne	national anthem
das Brandenburger Tor	Brandenburg Gate
der Kölner Dom	Cologne Cathedral
die geteilte Stadt	the divided city (Berlin)
die Mauer	the Wall
die Grenze	the border
die Bundeshauptstadt	Capital of (West) Germany

Bräuche   customs

die Lebensart	way of life
die Kultur	culture
die Küche	cooking
ein Gasthaus (n)	restaurant, inn
ein Gasthof (m)	restaurant, inn
der Weinbau	wine growing
ein Volksfest (n)	funfair
der Karneval	carnival
das Oktoberfest	Munich beer festival

See also Sections **25 CITY, 26 CARS, 38 PLANNING A HOLIDAY, 39 RAILWAYS, 40 FLYING, 41 PUBLIC TRANSPORT, 42 HOTEL, 43 CAMPING, 44 SEASIDE, 45 GEOGRAPHICAL TERMS** *and* **64 DIRECTIONS.**

50. ZWISCHENFÄLLE
INCIDENTS

geschehen	to happen
passieren	to happen
vorkommen	to occur
stattfinden	to take place
treffen	to meet
zusammentreffen	to coincide
vermissen	to miss
sich (wieder)finden	to find oneself
fehlen	to be missing
fallenlassen	to drop, to let go of
verschütten	to spill
umstoßen	to knock over
fallen	to fall
verderben	to spoil
beschädigen	to damage
brechen	to break
zerbrechen	to break
verursachen	to cause
vorsichtig sein	to be careful
bekommen	to get
kriegen	to get
vergessen	to forget
liegenlassen	to leave
verlieren	to lose
suchen	to look for
versuchen	to try
erkennen	to recognize
finden	to find
wiederfinden	to find (again)
sich verirren	to get lost
sich verlaufen	to get lost
vom Weg abkommen	to lose one's way
nach dem Weg fragen	to ask one's way

zerstreut	absent-minded
ungeschickt	clumsy
unerwartet	unexpected
zufällig	by chance
ungewollt	inadvertently
unbeabsichtigt	inadvertently
glücklicherweise	luckily, fortunately
unglücklicherweise	unfortunately
ein Zufall (*m*)	coincidence
der Zufall	chance
eine Überraschung	surprise
das Glück	luck, chance
das Pech	bad luck
ein Mißgeschick (*n*)	misadventure
ein Zusammentreffen (*n*)	meeting, encounter
eine Verabredung	date, meeting
die Rücksichtslosigkeit	heedlessness
der Schaden	damage
die Vergeßlichkeit	forgetfulness
der Verlust	loss
das Fundbüro	lost property office
eine Belohnung	reward

was ist los?
what's up?

welch ein Zufall!
what a coincidence!

ich habe eben immer Pech!
just my luck!

es hat geklappt/nicht geklappt
it worked/didn't work

Achtung!
watch out!

Vorsicht!
careful!

51. UNFÄLLE
ACCIDENTS

fahren	to drive, to go
die Vorfahrt nicht beachten	not to give way
ein Rotlicht (n) überfahren	to go through a red light
ein Stoppschild (n) überfahren	to ignore a stop sign
ins Schleudern geraten	to skid
platzen	to burst
die Kontrolle über das Fahrzeug verlieren	to lose control of the vehicle
sich überschlagen	to somersault
fahren gegen	to run into
überfahren	to run over
demolieren	to wreck, to demolish
beschädigen	to damage
zerstören	to wreck, to destroy
eingeschlossen sein	to be trapped
unter Schock (dat) stehen	to be in a state of shock
das Bewußtsein verlieren	to lose consciousness
das Bewußtsein wiedererlangen	to regain consciousness
im Koma liegen	to be in a coma
sterben	to die
umkommen	to die
ums Leben kommen	to be killed
miterleben	to witness
einen Bericht anfertigen	to draw up a report
entschädigen	to compensate
entgleisen	to be derailed
schiffbrüchig werden	to be shipwrecked
ausrutschen	to slip
ertrinken	to drown
ersticken	to suffocate
fallen (von)	to fall (from)

aus dem Fenster stürzen	to fall out of the window
einen elektrischen Schlag bekommen	to get an electric shock
durch einen Stromschlag ums Leben kommen	to electrocute oneself
sich verbrennen	to burn oneself
sich verbrühen	to scald oneself
sich schneiden	to cut oneself
betrunken	drunk
verletzt	injured
leicht verletzt	slightly injured
schwer verletzt	seriously injured
tot	dead
ernst	serious
versichert	insured

Verkehrsunfälle — road accidents

ein Unfall (m)	accident
ein Autounfall (m)	car accident
ein Verkehrsunfall (m)	road accident
die Straßenverkehrsordnung	Highway Code
ein Zusammenstoß (m)	car crash
eine Massenkarambolage	pile-up
der Aufprall	impact
eine Explosion	explosion
eine Geschwindigkeits- überschreitung	speeding
eine Alkoholkontrolle	breath test
Alkohol am Steuer	drunken driving
die Müdigkeit	fatigue
die schlechte Sicht	poor visibility
der Nebel	fog
der Regen	rain
das Glatteis	black ice
ein Abhang (m)	cliff, precipice
der Schaden	damage

andere Unfälle

other accidents

ein Arbeitsunfall (m)
ein Flugzeugabsturz (m)
eine Entgleisung
ein Bergunfall (m)
der Sturz
das Ertrinken
ein Stromschlag (m)

industrial accident
plane crash
derailment
mountaineering accident
fall
drowning
electric shock

Verletzte und Unfallzeugen

injured persons and witnesses

ein Verletzter, eine Verletzte
ein Schwerverletzter, eine Schwerverletzte
ein Toter, eine Tote
ein Zeuge, eine Zeugin
ein Augenzeuge, eine Augenzeugin

injured person
seriously injured person

dead person
witness
eye witness

eine Gehirnerschütterung
eine Verletzung
eine Verbrennung
der Blutverlust
die Beherrschung

concussion
injury
burn
loss of blood
composure

Hilfe

help

Notdienste (pl)
die Polizei
die Feuerwehr
die Erste Hilfe
ein Notfall (m)
ein Krankenwagen (m)
ein Arzt (m)
eine Krankenschwester
ein Krankenpfleger (m)

emergency services
police
fire brigade
first aid
emergency
ambulance
doctor
nurse
male nurse

die Sanitätsausrüstung	first aid kit
eine Trage	stretcher
die künstliche Beatmung	artificial respiration
die Mund-zu-Mund-Beatmung	kiss of life
der Sauerstoff	oxygen
ein Feuerlöscher (m)	extinguisher
der Pannendienst	breakdown service
der Rettungsdienst	rescue services

die Folgen — the consequences

der Schaden	damage
ein Bericht (m)	report
eine Geldstrafe	fine
der Führerscheinentzug	loss of one's driving licence
die Gerechtigkeit	justice
das Urteil	sentence
die Versicherung	insurance
die Verantwortung	responsibility

seine Bremsen haben versagt
his brakes failed

er ist mit ein paar Kratzern davongekommen
he escaped with only a few scratches

mein Auto hat Totalschaden
my car is a write-off

ihm ist der Führerschein entzogen worden
he lost his driving licence

See also Sections **6 HEALTH, 26 CARS, 28 WEATHER** *and* **52 DISASTERS**.

52. KATASTROPHEN
DISASTERS

angreifen	to attack
verteidigen	to defend
zusammenbrechen	to collapse
verhungern	to starve
ausbrechen	to erupt
explodieren	to explode
zittern	to shake
ersticken	to suffocate
verbrennen	to burn
löschen	to extinguish
den Alarm auslösen	to raise the alarm
retten	to rescue
sinken	to sink

Krieg

war

die Armee	army
die Marine	navy
die Luftwaffe	air force
der Feind	enemy
ein Verbündeter (*m*)	ally
das Schlachtfeld	battlefield
die Bombardierung	bombing
eine Bombe	bomb
eine Atombombe	atomic bomb
eine H-Bombe	hydrogen bomb
eine Granate	shell
eine Rakete	missile
ein Panzer (*m*)	tank
ein Gewehr (*n*)	gun
ein Maschinengewehr (*n*)	machine-gun
ein MG (*n*)	machine-gun
eine Mine	mine
Zivilisten (*pl*)	civilians

ein Soldat (*m*)	soldiers
ein General (*m*)	general
ein Oberst (*m*)	colonel
ein Feldwebel (*m*)	sergeant
ein Kapitän (*m*)	captain
die Grausamkeit	cruelty
die Folter	torture
der Tod	death
eine Wunde	wound
eine Verwundung	wound
ein Opfer (*n*)	victim, casualty
der Krieg	war
ein Luftschutzbunker (*m*)	air-raid shelter
ein Atombunker (*m*)	nuclear shelter
der radioaktive Niederschlag	radioactive fallout
ein Waffenstillstand (*m*)	truce
ein Vertrag (*m*)	treaty
der Sieg	victory
die Niederlage	defeat
der Frieden	peace

Naturkatastrophen   natural disasters

eine Dürre	drought
eine Hungersnot	famine
die Unterernährung	malnutrition
der Mangel an (+*dat*)	lack of
eine Epidemie	epidemic
ein Tornado (*m*)	tornado
ein Wirbelsturm (*m*)	cyclone
eine Flutwelle	tidal wave
eine Überschwemmung	flood
ein Erdbeben (*n*)	earthquake
ein Vulkan (*m*)	volcano
ein Vulkanausbruch (*m*)	volcanic eruption
die Lava	lava
eine Lawine	avalanche
eine Hilfsorganisation	relief organisation

das Rote Kreuz	Red Cross
ein Freiwilliger (*m*)	volunteer
die Rettung	rescue
ein SOS (*n*)	SOS

Feuer

fires

ein Feuer (*n*)	fire
der Rauch	smoke
Flammen (*pl*)	flames
eine Explosion	explosion
die Feuerwehr	fire brigade
ein Feuerwehrmann (*m*)	fireman
ein Feuerwehrauto (*n*)	fire engine
eine Leiter	ladder
ein Schlauch (*m*)	hose
der Notausgang	emergency exit
die Panik	panic
ein Krankenwagen (*m*)	ambulance
ein Notfall (*m*)	emergency
die Hilfe	help
die künstliche Beatmung	artificial respiration
ein Überlebender, eine Überlebende	survivor

"Hilfe!"
'help!'

"Feuer!"
'fire!'

See also Section **51 ACCIDENTS**.

53. VERBRECHEN
CRIMES

stehlen	to steal
klauen	to pinch
einbrechen	to burgle
überfallen	to attack (and rob), to mug
ermorden	to assassinate
töten	to kill
erstechen	to stab (to death)
erwürgen	to strangle (to death)
schießen	to shoot
erschießen	to shoot dead
vergiften	to poison
angreifen	to attack
bedrohen	to threaten
zwingen	to force
vergewaltigen	to rape
betrügen	to swindle
unterschlagen	to embezzle
spionieren	to spy
sich prostituieren	to prostitute oneself
mit Drogen betäuben	to drug
entführen	to kidnap, to abduct
kidnappen	to kidnap
Geiseln nehmen	to take hostages
in Brand setzen	to set fire to
festnehmen	to arrest
untersuchen	to investigate
eine Untersuchung durchführen	to lead an investigation
befragen	to question, to interrogate
durchsuchen	to search
zusammenschlagen	to beat up
einsperren	to imprison
umzingeln	to surround
abriegeln	to seal off

retten	to rescue
verteidigen	to defend
beschuldigen	to accuse
eine Klage einreichen	to take legal action
vor Gericht (*acc*) **stellen**	to judge, to try
beweisen	to prove
verurteilen	to sentence, to convict
freisprechen	to acquit
dürfen	to be allowed to
schuldig	guilty
unschuldig	innocent

Verbrechen

crime

ein Diebstahl (*m*)	theft
ein Raub (*m*)	robbery
ein Einbruch (*m*)	burglary, break-in
ein Raubüberfall (*m*)	hold-up
ein Überfall (*m*)	attack
ein bewaffneter Überfall	armed robbery, armed attack
ein Mord (*m*)	murder
ein Betrug (*m*)	fraud
ein Schwindel (*m*)	confidence trick
eine Erpressung	blackmail
eine Vergewaltigung	rape
die Prostitution	prostitution
die Zuhälterei	procuring
der Drogenhandel	drug trafficking
der Schmuggel	smuggling
die Spionage	spying
eine Geisel	hostage
ein(e) Mörder(in)	murderer
ein(e) Dieb(in)	thief
ein Taschendieb (*m*)	pickpocket
ein(e) Einbrecher(in)	burglar
ein(e) Erpresser(in)	blackmailer
ein Zuhälter (*m*)	pimp

ein **Drogenhändler** (m)	drug dealer
ein **Brandstifter** (m)	arsonist

Waffen

weapons

eine **Pistole**	pistol
ein **Revolver** (m)	gun, revolver
ein **Gewehr** (n)	gun, rifle
ein **Messer** (n)	knife
ein **Dolch** (m)	dagger
das **Gift**	poison
ein **Schlag** (m)	punch

die Polizei

police

ein **Polizist** (m)	policeman
ein **Polizeibeamter** (m)	policeman
ein **Bereitschaftspolizist** (m)	riot policeman
ein **Detektiv** (m)	detective
ein **Kommissar** (m)	superintendent
die **Polizeiwache**	police station
das **Polizeipräsidium**	police headquarters
ein **Bericht** (m)	report
Nachforschungen (pl)	investigations
eine **Untersuchung**	enquiry
ein **Polizeihund** (m)	police dog
ein(e) **Informant(in)**	informer
ein **Spitzel** (m)	informer, grass
ein **Gummiknüppel** (m)	truncheon
Handschellen (pl)	handcuffs
ein **Helm** (m)	helmet
ein **Schild** (m)	shield
das **Tränengas**	tear gas
ein **Polizeiauto** (n)	police van
ein **Streifenwagen** (m)	patrol car
eine **Zelle**	cell

die Justiz   the judicial system

der Prozeß	trial
ein Angeklagter, eine Angeklagte	accused
das Opfer	victim
ein Beweis (*m*)	proof
ein Zeuge, eine Zeugin	witness
ein Rechtsanwalt, eine Rechtsanwältin	lawyer
der Richter	judge
ein Schöffe, eine Schöffin	jury member
die Verteidigung	defence
das Urteil	sentence
ein Strafaufschub (*m*)	reprieve
ein Urteil (*n*) mit Bewährung	suspended sentence
ein mildes Urteil	lenient sentence
ein hartes Urteil	severe sentence
eine Geldstrafe	fine
das Gefängnis	imprisonment, prison
die lebenslängliche Freiheitsstrafe	life sentence
die Todesstrafe	death sentence
der elektrische Stuhl	electric chair
der Tod durch den Strang	hanging
ein Justizirrtum (*m*)	miscarriage of justice

er wurde zu zwanzig Jahren Gefängnis verurteilt
he was sentenced to 20 years' imprisonment

54. ABENTEUER UND TRÄUME
ADVENTURES AND DREAMS

spielen	to play
sich amüsieren	to have fun
sich (*dat*) vorstellen	to imagine
geschehen	to happen
sich verstecken	to hide
weglaufen	to run off
entkommen	to escape
verfolgen	to chase
entdecken	to discover
erforschen	to explore
wagen	to dare
vorsichtig sein	to be careful
sich verkleiden (als)	to dress up (as a)
die Schule schwänzen	to play truant
Versteck spielen	to play hide-and-seek
sich aus dem Staub machen	to take to one's heels
verzaubern	to bewitch
wahrsagen	to tell fortunes
vorhersagen	to foretell
träumen	to dream
einen Traum haben	to have a dream
einen Alptraum haben	to have a nightmare

Abenteuer   adventures

ein Abenteuer (*n*)	adventure
ein Mißgeschick (*n*)	misadventure
ein Spiel (*n*)	game
ein Spielplatz (*m*)	playground
eine Reise	journey
eine Flucht	escape
eine Verkleidung	disguise

das Unbekannte	unknown
ein Ereignis (n)	event
eine Entdeckung	discovery
der Zufall	chance
das Glück	luck
das Pech	bad luck
die Gefahr	danger
die Lebensgefahr	serious danger
ein Risiko (n)	risk
ein Versteck (n)	hiding place
eine Höhle	cave
eine Insel	island
ein Schatz (m)	treasure
der Mut	courage
der Leichtsinn	recklessness
die Feigheit	cowardice

Märchen und Sagen   fairytales and legends

ein Zauberer (m)	wizard, magician
eine Hexe	witch
eine Fee	fairy
ein Hexenmeister (m)	sorcerer
ein Wahrsager (m)	prophet, seer
ein Gnom (m)	gnome
ein Kobold (m)	imp, goblin
ein Zwerg (m)	dwarf
ein Riese (m)	giant
ein Geist (m)	ghost
ein Gespenst (m)	ghost
ein Skelett (m)	skeleton
ein Vampir (m)	vampire
ein Drache (m)	dragon
ein Werwolf (m)	werewolf
ein Ungeheuer (n)	monster
ein außerirdisches Wesen	extra-terrestrial
eine Eule	owl
eine Kröte	toad
eine schwarze Katze	black cat

ein Spukschloß (*n*)	haunted castle
ein Friedhof (*m*)	cemetery
ein Raumschiff (*n*)	space ship
ein Ufo (*n*)	UFO
das Universum	universe
die Magie	magic
der Aberglaube	superstition
ein Zauberstab (*m*)	magic wand
ein fliegender Teppich	flying carpet
der Besenstiel	broomstick
eine Glaskugel	crystal ball
das Tarock	tarot
Handlinien (*pl*)	lines of the hand
der Vollmond	full moon

Träume   dreams

ein Traum (*m*)	dream
ein Tagtraum (*m*)	daydream
die Tagträumerei	daydreaming
ein Alptraum (*m*)	nightmare
die Einbildung	imagination
das Unterbewußtsein	subconscious
eine Halluzination	hallucination
das Erwachen	awakening

ich hatte einen schönen Traum/einen furchtbaren Alptraum
I've had a nice dream/horrible nightmare

weißt du, was mir gestern passiert ist?
do you know what happened to me yesterday?

du hast zuviel Phantasie
you've got too much imagination

55. DIE ZEIT
THE TIME

Zeitmesser	things that tell the time
eine Uhr	watch, clock
eine Armbanduhr	wristwatch
eine Digitaluhr	digital clock/watch
ein Wecker (m)	alarm clock
eine Stoppuhr	stopwatch
die Zeitansage	speaking clock
das Klingeln	ringing
der Glockenturm	bell tower
die Glocke	bell
die Sonnenuhr	sun dial
die Eieruhr	eggtimer
Zeiger (pl)	hands of a watch
der Stundenzeiger	hour hand
der Minutenzeiger	minute hand
der Sekundenzeiger	second hand
die Zeitzone	time zone

wie spät ist es?	what time is it?
ein Uhr	one o'clock
acht Uhr (morgens)	eight am, eight o'clock in the morning
fünf nach acht	five (minutes) past eight
viertel nach acht	a quarter past eight
halb elf	ten thirty, half past ten
fünf nach halb elf	twenty-five to eleven
zwanzig vor elf	twenty to eleven
viertel vor elf	a quarter to eleven

zwei Uhr (nachmittags)	two pm, two o'clock in the afternoon
vierzehn Uhr	two pm
vierzehn Uhr dreißig	two thirty pm
zehn Uhr (abends)	ten pm, ten o'clock in the evening
zweiundzwanzig Uhr	ten pm

Zeiteinteilungen — divisions of time

die Zeit	time
ein Augenblick (*m*)	moment, instant
ein Moment (*m*)	moment
eine Sekunde	second
eine Minute	minute
eine Viertelstunde	quarter of an hour
eine halbe Stunde	half an hour
eine Dreiviertelstunde	three quarters of an hour
eine Stunde	hour
eineinhalb Stunden	an hour and a half
ein Tag (*m*)	day
der Sonnenaufgang	sunrise
der Morgen	morning
der Vormittag	morning
der Mittag	noon
der Nachmittag	afternoon
der Abend	evening
der Sonnenuntergang	sunset
die Nacht	night
Mitternacht	midnight

pünktlich/zu spät kommen — being on time/late

zu früh kommen	to be (too) early
pünktlich sein	to be on time
pünktlich ankommen	to arrive on time
zu spät kommen	to be late

Verspätung haben	to be late
rechtzeitig kommen	to arrive in time
es eilig haben	to be in a hurry
sich beeilen	to hurry (up)

wann?   when?

wann	when
seit	since
als	when
vor (+dat)	before
nach	after
während	during
früh	early
spät	late
später	later
schon	already
jetzt	now
im Moment	at the moment
sofort	immediately, straight away
sogleich	straight away
plötzlich	suddenly
zur Zeit	presently
vor kurzem	a short while ago
bald	soon
dann	then (*next*)
damals	then (*at that time*)
schließlich	finally
zu der Zeit	at that time
kürzlich	recently
währenddessen	meanwhile
lange Zeit	for a long time
vor langer Zeit	a long time ago
immer	always
nie(mals)	never
manchmal	sometimes
oft	often
von Zeit zu Zeit	from time to time
kaum jemals	rarely

wieviel Uhr ist es?
what time is it?

es ist zwei Uhr
it's two o'clock

können Sie mir die (genaue) Zeit sagen?
do you have the (exact) time?

um wieviel Uhr fährt der Zug ab?
at what time does the train leave?

es ist etwa zwei Uhr
it's about two o'clock

es ist genau neun Uhr
it's nine o'clock exactly

er kommt erst um halb sechs
he's not coming until half past five

meine Uhr geht vor
my watch is fast

meine Uhr geht nach
my watch is slow

ich habe meine Uhr gestellt
I've set my watch to the right time

wir sind spät dran
we're late

haben Sie Zeit, mit ihm zu sprechen?
do you have time to speak to him?

ich habe keine Zeit um auszugehen
I haven't time to go out

es ist noch nicht soweit
it's not time yet

56. DIE WOCHE
THE WEEK

Montag	Monday
Dienstag	Tuesday
Mittwoch	Wednesday
Donnerstag	Thursday
Freitag	Friday
Samstag	Saturday
Sonnabend	Saturday
Sonntag	Sunday
der Tag (*m*)	day
die Woche	week
das Wochenende	weekend
acht Tage	a week
zwei Wochen	a fortnight
vierzehn Tage	a fortnight
heute	today
morgen	tomorrow
übermorgen	the day after tomorrow
gestern	yesterday
vorgestern	the day before yesterday
am Vortag	the day before
am nächsten Tag	the day after
am übernächsten Tag	two days later
diese Woche	this week
nächste Woche	next week
letzte Woche	last week
vorige Woche	last week
vergangene Woche	last week
letzten Montag	last Monday
vorigen Montag	last Monday
nächsten Montag	next Monday
montags	on Mondays
montagsmorgens	on Monday mornings
montagsabends	on Monday evenings

heute in einer Woche	in a week's time, a week today
heute in vierzehn Tagen	in two weeks' time
Donnerstag in einer Woche	Thursday week
gestern morgen	yesterday morning
gestern abend	last night, yesterday evening
heute Abend	this evening, tonight
diese/heute Nacht	last night, tonight
morgen früh	tomorrow morning
morgen abend	tomorrow evening
vor drei Tagen	three days ago

am Sonntag gehe ich zum Gottesdienst/zur Messe
on Sunday I go to church/mass

donnerstags gehe ich ins Schwimmbad
on Thursdays I go to the swimming pool

er besucht mich jeden Tag
he comes to see me every day

bis morgen!
see you tomorrow!

bis nächste Woche!
see you next week!

innerhalb drei Tagen
(with)in three days

57. DAS JAHR
THE YEAR

Monate	months of the year
Januar	January
Februar	February
März	March
April	April
Mai	May
Juni	June
Juli	July
August	August
September	September
Oktober	October
November	November
Dezember	December
ein Monat (*m*)	month
ein Jahr (*n*)	year
ein Schuljahr (*n*)	school year
ein Jahrzehnt (*n*)	decade
ein Jahrhundert (*n*)	century
ein Jahrtausend (*n*)	thousand years, millenium

Jahreszeiten	seasons
die Jahreszeit	season
der Frühling	spring
der Sommer	summer
der Herbst	autumn
der Winter	winter

Feiertage	festivals
ein Feiertag (*m*)	holiday (*one day*)

Weihnachten	Christmas
Neujahr	New Year's Day
Silvester	New Year's Eve
Ostern	Easter
der Karfreitag	Good Friday
der Rosenmontag	Monday before Ash Wednesday
der Aschermittwoch	Ash Wednesday
Pfingsten	Whitsun
Allerheiligen	All Saints' Day
der Tag der Deutschen Einheit	German national holiday (*17th June*)
der Geburtstag	birthday
der Namenstag	name day
der Valentinstag	St Valentine's Day
der erste April	April Fools' Day

ich habe im Februar Geburtstag
my birthday is in February

im März regnet es viel
it rains a lot in March

ich mag den Sommer am liebsten
summer is my favourite season

im Winter gehe ich Skilaufen
in winter I go skiing

58. DAS DATUM
THE DATE

zurückgehen auf (+*acc*)	to date from, to go back to
dauern	to last
die Vergangenheit	past
die Zukunft	future
die Gegenwart	present
die Geschichte	history
die Vorgeschichte	prehistory
die Antike	antiquity
das Mittelalter	Middle Ages
das zwanzigste Jahrhundert	twentieth century
das Jahr 2000	year 2000
das Datum	date
aktuell	present, current
modern	modern
gegenwärtig	present
vergangen	past
zukünftig	future
jährlich	annual, yearly
monatlich	monthly
wöchentlich	weekly
täglich	daily
früher	in the past, formerly
damals	then, at that time
in der Vergangenheit	in the past
lange Zeit	for a long time
niemals	never
immer	always
manchmal	sometimes
als	when
wenn	when
seit	since
noch	again, still

zu der Zeit	at that time
vor Christus (v.Chr.)	BC
nach Christus (n.Chr.)	AD

welches Datum ist heute?/den wievielten haben wir heute?
what date is it today?

es ist der 1./erste Juni 1988/neunzehnhundert-achtundachtzig
it's the first of June 1988

im Jahre 1990/neunzehnhundertneunzig
in 1990

es ist der 15./fünfzehnte August
it's the fifteenth of August

Bonn, den 5. April 1986
Bonn, 5th of April 1986

er kommt am 16. Juli zurück
he'll be back on the 16th of July

er ist vor einem Jahr gegangen
he left a year ago

als er da war
when he was there

wenn er zurückkommt
when he comes back

seit ich hier wohne
since I've been living here

es war einmal ...
once upon a time, there was ...

See also Section **57** *YEAR*.

59. ZAHLEN
NUMBERS

null	zero
eins	one
zwei	two
drei	three
vier	four
fünf	five
sechs	six
sieben	seven
acht	eight
neun	nine
zehn	ten
elf	eleven
zwölf	twelve
dreizehn	thirteen
vierzehn	fourteen
fünfzehn	fifteen
sechzehn	sixteen
siebzehn	seventeen
achtzehn	eighteen
neunzehn	nineteen
zwanzig	twenty
einundzwanzig	twenty-one
zweiundzwanzig	twenty-two
dreißig	thirty
vierzig	forty
fünfzig	fifty
sechzig	sixty
siebzig	seventy
achtzig	eighty
neunzig	ninety
(ein)hundert	hundred
(ein)hundert(und)eins	hundred and one
(ein)hundert(und)zweiund- sechzig	hundred and sixty-two
zweihundert	two hundred

zweihundert(und)zwei	two hundred and two
(ein)tausend	thousand
zweitausend	two thousand
zehntausend	ten thousand
hunderttausend	hundred thousand
eine Million	million
erste	first
letzte	last
zweite	second
dritte	third
vierte	fourth
fünfte	fifth
sechste	sixth
siebte	seventh
achte	eighth
neunte	ninth
zehnte	tenth
elfte	eleventh
zwölfte	twelfth
dreizehnte	thirteenth
vierzehnte	fourteenth
fünfzehnte	fifteenth
sechzehnte	sixteenth
siebzehnte	seventeenth
achtzehnte	eighteenth
neunzehnte	nineteenth
zwanzigste	twentieth
einundzwanzigste	twenty-first
zweiundzwanzigste	twenty-second
dreißigste	thirtieth
vierzigste	fortieth
fünfzigste	fiftieth
sechzigste	sixtieth
siebzigste	seventieth
achtzigste	eightieth
neunzigste	ninetieth
hundertste	hundredth
hundert(und)erste	hundred and first
hundertzwanzigste	hundred and twentieth

zweihundertste	two hundredth
tausendste	thousandth
zweitausendste	two thousandth
die Ziffer	figure
die Zahl	number
die Nummer	number (*telephone, house etc*)

hundert/tausend Mark
a/one hundred/thousand marks

der/die/das achte und der/die/das elfte
the eighth and the eleventh

eine große Zahl von Schülern
a large number of pupils

zwei Komma drei (2,3)
two point three (2.3)

eine Million Schweizer Franken
one million Swiss francs

60. MENGEN
QUANTITIES

berechnen	to calculate
zählen	to count
wiegen	to weigh
messen	to measure
teilen	to divide
verteilen	to distribute, to share out
füllen	to fill
leeren	to empty
wegnehmen	to remove
vermindern	to lessen, to reduce
erhöhen	to increase
hinzufügen	to add
genügen	to be enough
nichts	nothing
alles	everything
aller/alle/alles ...	all the ..., the whole ...
jeder/jede/jedes ...	all the ..., every ...
etwas	something, some
einige	several, some
jeder	everybody
alle (*pl*)	everybody
ein bißchen	a little (bit of)
ein wenig	a little (bit of)
wenig	few
viel	a lot (of), much
viele	a lot of, many
kein(e) ...	no ..., not any ...
keine ... mehr	no more ...
mehr	more
weniger	less
der/die/das meiste	most
genug	enough
zuviel	too much
zu viele	too many

etwa	about
ungefähr	about
mehr oder weniger	more or less
kaum	scarcely
gerade	just
völlig	absolutely
höchstens	at the most
wieder	again
nur	only
mindestens	at least
die Hälfte	half
ein Viertel (*n*)	a quarter (of)
ein Drittel (*n*)	a third
und ein halb	and a half
anderthalb	one and a half
eineinhalb	one and a half
zwei Drittel	two thirds
drei Viertel	three quarters
das ganze	the whole
selten	rare
häufig	numerous
unzählig	innumerable
genug	enough
überflüssig	excessive
gleich	equal
ungleich	unequal
voll	full
leer	empty
einfach	single
zweifach	double
doppelt	double
dreifach	treble
eine Menge	lots (of)
ein Haufen (*m*)	a stack (of)
ein Stück (*n*)	a piece (of)
ein Glas (*n*)	a glass (of)
eine Flasche	a bottle (of)
eine Dose	a box/tin (of)
ein Paket (*n*)	a packet (of)

ein Bissen (*m*)	a mouthful (of) (*food*)
ein Schluck (*m*)	a mouthful (of) (*drink*), a swallow
ein Löffel (*m*)	a spoonful (of)
eine Handvoll	a handful (of)
ein Paar (*n*)	a pair (of)
ein paar	a couple (of)
eine große Zahl von	a large number of
der (An)teil	share
ein Teil (*n*) (von)	part (of)
ein Dutzend (*n*)	dozen
hunderte	hundreds
tausende	thousands
die übrigen	the rest/remainder
die Menge	quantity
die Zahl	number
der Durchschnitt	average
das Gewicht	weight

Maße und Gewichte

weights and measurements

ein Gramm (*n*)	gramme
ein Pfund (*n*)	half kilo
ein Kilo (*n*)	kilo
ein Zentner (*m*)	50 kilos
eine Tonne	1000 kg, tonne
ein Liter (*m*)	litre
ein Millimeter (*m*)	millimetre
ein Zentimeter (*m*)	centimetre
ein Meter (*m*)	metre
ein Kilometer (*m*)	kilometre
eine Meile	mile

See also Section **59 NUMBERS**.

61. BESCHREIBUNG VON DINGEN
DESCRIBING THINGS

ein Ding (n)	thing
eine Art (von)	a kind of
die Größe	size
der Umfang	size
die Breite	width, breadth
die Höhe	height
die Tiefe	depth
die Schönheit	beauty
die Häßlichkeit	ugliness
die Form	shape
die Gestalt	shape
die Eigenschaft	quality
der Vorteil	advantage
der Nachteil	disadvantage
groß	tall, big, large
klein	small
riesig	enormous
winzig	tiny
mikroskopisch klein	microscopic
breit	wide
schmal	narrow
eng	narrow, small
dick	thick, large, fat
dünn	thin, slim
flach	flat, shallow
tief	deep
lang	long
kurz	short
hoch	high
niedrig	low
steil	steep
schön	lovely, beautiful

gut	good, well
besser	better
am besten	the best
wichtig	important
hauptsächlich	main
hübsch	pretty
wunderbar	marvellous
sehenswert	worth seeing
großartig	magnificent, superb
beeindruckend	imposing
phantastisch	fantastic
prima	great
klasse	terrific
bemerkenswert	remarkable
überraschend	surprising
außergewöhnlich	exceptional
ausgezeichnet	excellent
perfekt	perfect
normal	normal
unterschiedlich	varied
seltsam	strange
komisch	strange, funny
häßlich	ugly
schlecht	bad(ly)
schlechter	worse
am schlechtesten	the worst
mittelmäßig	mediocre
furchtbar	abominable
entsetzlich	appalling
schrecklich	dreadful
grauenvoll	atrocious
unmöglich	impossible
leicht	light
schwer	heavy
hart	hard
fest	firm
solide	solid
stabil	sturdy
weich	soft

zart	tender
fein	fine, delicate
zerbrechlich	fragile
glatt	smooth
rauh	rough
warm	warm
heiß	hot
kalt	cold
kühl	cool
lauwarm	lukewarm, tepid
trocken	dry
naß	wet
feucht	damp
flüssig	liquid, runny
einfach	simple
kompliziert	complicated
schwierig	difficult
leicht	easy
möglich	possible
unmöglich	impossible
praktisch	practical, handy
nützlich	useful
nutzlos	useless
alt	old
uralt	ancient
neu	new
modern	modern
veraltet	out of date
altmodisch	old-fashioned
frisch	fresh, cool
sauber	clean
schmutzig	dirty
dreckig	filthy
widerlich	disgusting
gebogen	curved
gerade	straight
rund	round, circular
oval	oval

rechteckig	rectangular
quadratisch	square
viereckig	square, rectangular, four-sided
dreieckig	triangular
länglich	oblong
sehr	very
zu	too
ziemlich	rather
ganz	quite
von erstklassiger Qualität	of top quality
von schlechter Qualität	of poor quality

was ist das?
what's that?

wozu dient das?
what's it for?

das ist ja kinderleicht
it's child's play

See also Section **62 COLOURS**.

62. FARBEN
COLOURS

die Farbe	colour
beige	beige
blau	blue
blond	blond
braun	brown
fleischfarben	flesh-coloured
gelb	yellow
golden	gold, golden
grau	grey
grün	green
himmelblau	sky blue
kastanienbraun	chestnut
lila	purple
orange(farben)	orange
purpur(rot)	crimson
rosa	pink
rot	red
schwarz	black
silbern	silver
türkis	turquoise
violett	purple
weiß	white
lebhaft	vivid
blaß	pale
einfarbig	self-coloured
uni(farben)	plain
mehrfarbig	multicoloured
bunt	(multi)coloured
hell	light
dunkel	dark
hellgrün	light green
dunkelgrün	dark green

63. STOFFE UND MATERIALIEN
MATERIALS

echt	real
natürlich	natural
synthetisch	synthetic
künstlich	artificial
das Material	material, substance
die Zusammensetzung	composition
der Stoff	material, cloth
das Rohmaterial	raw material
ein Produkt (*n*)	product
die Erde	earth
das Wasser	water
die Luft	air
das Feuer	fire
der Stein	stone
der Fels	rock
das Erz	ore
das Mineral	mineral
ein Edelstein (*m*)	precious stone
das Kristall	crystal
der Marmor	marble
der Granit	granite
der Diamant	diamond
der Ton	clay
das Öl	oil, petroleum
das Gas	gas
das Erdgas	natural gas
das Metall	metal
das Aluminium	aluminium
die Bronze	bronze
das Kupfer	copper
das Messing	brass
der Zinn	tin, pewter
das Eisen	iron

der Stahl	steel
das Blei	lead
das Gold	gold
das Silber	silver
das Holz	wood
das Rohr	cane, wickerwork
das Stroh	straw
der Bambus	bamboo
das Sperrholz	plywood
der Beton	concrete
der Zement	cement
der Backstein	brick
der Gips	plaster
der Kitt	putty
der Leim	glue
das Glas	glass
die Pappe	cardboard
das Papier	paper
das Plastik	plastic
das Gummi	rubber
das Wachs	wax
der Ton	earthenware
das Porzellan	porcelain, china
das Steingut	stoneware
der Sandstein	sandstone
das Leder	leather
das Wildleder	suede
der Pelz	fur
das Acryl	acrylic
die Baumwolle	cotton
die Spitze	lace
die Wolle	wool
das Leinen	linen
das Nylon	nylon
das Polyester	polyester
die reine Schurwolle	pure new wool
die Seide	silk

der Kunststoff	synthetic/man-made material
die Leinwand	canvas
das Wachstuch	oilcloth
der Tweed	tweed
die Kaschmirwolle	cashmere
der Samt	velvet
der Kord	cord
fest	solid
flüssig	liquid
gasförmig	gaseous
kupfern	copper
eisern	iron
bleiern	lead
golden	gold, golden
silbern	silver
steinern	stone
tönern	clay, earthenware
hölzern	wooden
gläsern	glass
ledern	leather
seiden	silk
wollen	woollen

dieses Haus ist aus Holz
this house is made of wood

64. RICHTUNGEN
DIRECTIONS

fragen	to ask
zeigen	to show
nehmen	to take, to follow
weitergehen/weiterfahren	to keep going
folgen	to follow
vorbeigehen/vorbeifahren an (+dat)	to go past
wenden	to turn
zurückgehen/zurückfahren	to go back
rückwärts fahren	to reverse
rechts abbiegen	to turn right
links abbiegen	to turn left

Richtungen
directions

links	(on the) left
rechts	(on the) right
nach links	to the left
nach rechts	to the right
geradeaus	straight ahead
wo ... hin	where ... to
wo ... her	where ... from

Himmels-richtungen
the points of the compass

der Norden	north
der Süden	south
der Osten	east
der Westen	west
der Nordosten	north-east
der Südwesten	south-west

der Kompaß	compass
ein Wegweiser (*m*)	signpost
wo	where
vor	in front of, before
hinter	behind
über	over
unter	under
neben	beside
gegenüber	opposite
mitten in (+*dat*)	in the middle of
entlang	along
am Ende	at the end
zwischen	between
irgendwo	somewhere
nach	to, after
hinter der Ampel	after the traffic lights
kurz vor (+*dat*)	just before
auf ... Meter	for ... metres
an der nächsten Kreuzung	at the next crossroads
die erste Straße rechts	first on the right
die zweite Straße links	second on the left

können Sie mir sagen, wie ich zum Bahnhof komme?
can you tell me how to get to the station?

fahren Sie geradeaus, biegen Sie dann links ab ...
go straight on, then turn left ...

ist es weit von hier?
is it far from here?

100 Meter entfernt
100 metres away

links vom Postamt
to the left of the post office

südlich von Mainz
south of Mainz

65. ABKÜRZUNGEN
ABBREVIATIONS

Abs. (Absender)	from (sender of letter *etc*)
betr. (betrifft)	re
bzw. (beziehungsweise)	or, that is
cm (Zentimeter)	cm
d.h. (das heißt)	i.e.
DM (Deutsche Mark)	DM (German mark)
einschl. (einschließlich)	incl.
ev. (evangelisch)	protestant
evtl. (eventuell)	possibly
Fr. (Frau)	Mrs, Ms
Frl. (Fräulein)	Miss, Ms
g (Gramm)	g
geb. (geboren)	born, née
gem. (gemäß)	according to
gez. (gezeichnet)	sig, signed
Hr. (Herr)	Mr
i.A. (im Auftrag)	pp (pro persona, on behalf of)
Jh. (Jahrhundert)	cent (century)
kath. (katholisch)	RC (catholic)
kg (Kilogramm)	kg
km (Kilometer)	km
mm (Millimeter)	mm
Nr. (Nummer)	No. (number)
od. (oder)	or
Pf. (Pfennig)	pfennig
Pfd. (Pfund)	lb (German pound − 500 grammes)
qm (Quadratmeter)	m^2 (square metres)
Std. (Stunde)	h (hour)
Str. (Straße)	St (street)
u. (und)	and
u.a. (unter anderem)	amongst other things
usw. (und so weiter)	etc
z.B. (zum Beispiel)	eg

INDEX

A levels 30
able 30
about 34, 60
above 64
abroad 49
absent 30
absolutely 34
accent 48
accept (to) 31
accident 51
accompany (to) 22
accuse (to) 53
active 11
activity 20
actor 10
address 8, 35
adore (to) 14
adult 9
advertisement 21
advise (to) 6
affectionately 11
after 55
afternoon 55
aftershave 3
again 60
against 32
age 9
agricultural 45
agriculture 27
air 63
airmail 35
airport 40
alive 6
all 60
allow (to) 11
allowed 26, 53
almost 34
alone 22
along 64
Alps 46

always 55, 58
ambitious 10
ambulance 51
American 47
amusing 11
ancient 61
angry 12
animal 27
ankle 4
announce 34
anorak 2
answer 30
answer (to) 30, 34
apologize (to) 37
appalling 61
appetite 13
apple 16
appliance 17
appointment 6
appreciate (to) 14
approve (to) 34
apricot 16
argue (to) 32
arithmetic 30
arm 4
armchair 23, 24
around 34
arrest (to) 53
arrival 39
arrive (to) 7, 41
art 30
article 21
ashtray 16, 24
asleep 5
aspirin 6
Atlantic 46
audience 22
aunt 29
Austria 46
Austrian 47

automatic 26
autumn 57
avenue 25

baby 29
back 4, 7, 41
backache 6
bad 11, 28, 61
badly 61
bag 18
baker 10
baker's 18
balcony 24
ball 19
ballet 22
Baltic 46
banana 16
bandage 6
bank 31
bank account 31
banker's card 31
banknote 31
bar 22
basement 24
basin 17
bath 15, 24
bathroom 24, 42
battery 26
Bavaria 46
beach 44
beat (to) 19, 20
beautiful 1, 61
because 34
become (to) 5
bed 23, 42
bedroom 24
bedside table 23
beef 16
beer 16

INDEX

beginning 7
behave (*to*) 11
behind 64
believe (*to*) 32
belt 2
beside 64
best 14
best wishes 37
better 6, 61
bicycle 19, 20
bidet 24
big 61
bill 22, 42
bin 24
biology 30
bird 27
birth 9
birthday 22, 37, 57
biscuit 16
black 1, 62
blanket 15
block of flats 24
blonde 3
blood 4
blouse 2
blue 62
boat 44
body 4
bomber jacket 2
book 20
book (*to*) 22, 38, 39
book of tickets 41
bookcase 23, 24
booking 39
bookshop 18
boot 26
boots 2
border 38
bored 20
boring 10
born 8, 9
boss 10
bottle 60
bottom 4
boulevard 25
bowl 17

boy 8
boyfriend 29
brake 26
bread 16
bread and butter 16
break 30
break (*to*) 50
break one's arm 6
breakdown 26
breakdown vehicle 51
breakfast 15, 16, 42
bridge 25
bring (*to*) 22
British 47
brochure 38
brother 29
brown 1, 3, 62
brush (*to*) 15
Brussels 46
budget 31
buffet 39
building 25
burn (*to*) 51
bus 41
bus station 41
business 10
but 34
butcher 10
butcher's 18
butter 16
button 2
buy (*to*) 18, 31
by 41

cabbage 16
café 22
cake 16
cake shop 18
call (*to*) 36
call back (*to*) 36
called 8
calm 11
Calorgaz 43
camera 20

camp (*to*) 43
camper 43
camping 43
campsite 43
Canada 46
Canadian 47
capital city 45
car 26
car crash 51
car ferry 44
car mechanic 26
car park 25
caravan 43
career 10
careful 54
carriage 39
cartoon 22
cashdesk 31
cassette 24
castle 25
cat 27
catch (*to*) 6
cathedral 25
Catholic 8
cauliflower 16
cellar 24
centimetre 60
central heating 24
centre 25
century 57
certificate 10, 30
chair 23, 24
champion 19
championship 19
change 18, 28
change (*to*) 28, 31, 41
changeable 28
channel 21
Channel 46
character 11
charming 11
cheap 18
check (*to*) 26
check in (*to*) 40
cheers 37
cheese 16

INDEX

chemist 10
chemist's 18
chemistry 30
chequebook 31
chest 4
chicken 16, 27
child 9, 29
chips 16
chocolate 16
choice 14
choir 20
choose (to) 18
Christmas 57
church 25
cider 16
cigar 16
cigarette 16
cine-camera 20
cinema 22
city 25
city centre 25
class 30, 39
classical music 22
classified ads 21
classroom 30
clean 61
clean (to) 17
clear the table (to) 17
cliff 45
climate 28
clinic 6
clock 55
close (to) 7
closed 42
clothes 2
cloud 28
cloudy 28
club 20
clutch 26
coach 41
coach (of train) 39
coast 44
coat 2
cobbler's 18
coffee 16

coin 31
coke 16
cold 6, 28, 61
colleague 10
collection 20
collection (of mail) 35
college 30
Cologne 46
colour 62
come (to) 7
come back (to) 7
come home (to) 15
comedian 10
comfortable 42
commercial 21
communism 33
communist 33
company 10
compartment 39
complain (to) 49
complaint 42
compliment 37
compulsory 26
computer 24
concert 22
confirm (to) 34
congratulations 37
connection 39
conservative 33
constipated 6
consulate 49
continent 45
continue (to) 7
convince (to) 34
cook (to) 17
cooker 17
corner 24
correspond (to) 35
cost (to) 18
cotton 63
cotton wool 6
cough mixture 6
council flat 24
count (to) 60
counter 31

country 45, 46
countryside 8
courage 54
cousin 29
cow 27
cream 16
credit 31
credit card 31
cricket 19
crisps 16
criticism 34
criticize (to) 34
cross (to) 26
crossroads 26
cry 12
cup 17
cupboard 23, 24
currency 31
curtain 23, 24
customer 18
customs 38
cut (to) 3, 17
cut oneself (to) 51
cutlery 17
cycling 19
cyclist 19, 26

dad 29
daily 58
dairy 18
damage 51
damp 61
dance 22
dance (to) 20
danger 54
dangerous 10
Danube 46
dare (to) 54
dark 62
date 58
date of birth 9
daughter 29
day 55, 56
day after 56
day after tomorrow 56

INDEX

day before 56
day before yesterday 56
day off 10
Dear Sir 35
death 6
decade 57
decide 14
declare (*to*) 38
decorator 10
deep 61
defend (*to*) 32
degree (*diploma*) 10
degree (*temperature*) 28
delay 40
delayed 40
delicatessen 18
delicious 13
delighted 11
democracy 33
democratic 33
dentist 6, 10
deodorant 3
department 18
department store 18
departure 39
depend 37
deposit 38
describe (*to*) 1
description 1
dessert 16
detest (*to*) 14
dial (*to*) 36
dialling tone 36
diarrhoea 6
diary 23
die (*to*) 6
difference 14
different 14
difficult 10, 61
dining hall 30
dining room 24, 42
dinner 15, 16
diploma 30
direction 41, 64

director 10
dirty 61
disappointed 12
disapprove (*to*) 11
disco 22
discussion 34
disgusting 61
dish 16
dishes 17
dislike (*to*) 14
district 25
disturb (*to*) 37
diversion 26
divorced 8
DIY 20
doctor 6, 10, 51
documentary 21
dog 27
door 24
dormitory 43
doubt (*to*) 34
downstairs 24
dozen 60
drawing 20, 30
dreadful 61
dress 2
drink 16
drink (*to*) 16
drinking water 43
drive (*to*) 26
driver 10, 26, 41
driving licence 26
drop (*to*) 50
drop off (*to*) 22
drown (*to*) 44, 51
dry 28
dry cleaning 18
duty doctor 6
duty-free 38

ear 4
early 55
earn (*to*) 10
east 64
Easter 57

East Germany 46
easy 10, 61
eat (*to*) 16
economy 33
education 30
egg 16
electrical 17
electrician 10
electricity 17
elegant 2
embassy 49
emergency exit 42
emergency services 51
employee 10
employer 10
employment 10
empty 60
encounter 50
end 7
engaged 8, 36
engine 26
England 46
English 47, 48
enjoy oneself (*to*) 20
enjoy your meal 37
enough 60
entirely 34
entrance 7, 24
envelope 35
equal 14
essential 61
etc 65
Eurocheque 31
Europe 46
European 47
evening 55
evening out 22
every 60
everybody 60
exaggerate (*to*) 34
examination 30
excellent 61
except 34
exceptional 61
excess fare 41

INDEX

exchange 49
exchange (to) 18
excursion 49
excuse 11
excuse me 37
exercise book 30
exist (to) 8
exit 41
expense 31
expensive 18
express train 39
eye 1, 4

face 4
face cream 3
factory 10, 25
factory worker 10
fair 3
fall (to) 50
fall asleep (to) 15
fall ill (to) 6
family 29
famous 49
far from 64
fascinating 20
fashion 2
fast 26
fast train 39
fat 1
father 29
favourite 14
Federal Republic of
  Germany 46
fed up 5
feel (to) 5
feel like (to) 14
ferry 44
festival 57
fetch (to) 7
few 60
field 27
fill (to) 60
fill up (to) 26
film (for camera) 20
film (movie) 21, 22

finally 55
find (to) 50
find a job (to) 10
find again (to) 50
find oneself (to) 50
fine 61
fine (money) 26, 51
finger 4
finish (to) 7
fire! 52
fireman 10, 51
first 59
first aid kit 51
first class 39
first name 8
firstly 55
fish 16, 27
fishing 19
flannel 15
flat 24
flat (tyre) 26
flavour 16
flight 40
floor 24
flower 27
flu 6
fluently 48
fly (to) 40
fog 28
follow (to) 7
food 16
foot 4
football 19
for 6, 32
for a long time 55,
  58
forbid (to) 11
forbidden 53
foreigner 32, 49
forest 27
forget (to) 38, 50
forgive (to) 11
fork 17
form 35
fortnight 56
fortunately 50

four-star petrol 26
frail 5
France 46
frankly 34
free (no charge) 18
free (toilet) 39
freezer 17
freezing 28
French 47, 48
fresh 16
FRG 46
fridge 17
friend 29
frightened 12
from 35, 39
from time to time 55
front 41
fruit 16
fruit juice 16
fruiterer 18
frying pan 17
fuel 26
full 60
full board 42
funny 11
furious 12
furnished (flat) 24
furniture 23, 24
future 10, 58

game 20, 23
garage (of house) 24
garage (for repairs)
  26
garage mechanic 10
garden 24
gas 17, 63
gas cooker 17
GDR 46
gear 26
generally 34
gentleman 8
geography 30
German 47, 48
German class 30

INDEX

German Democratic Republic 46
German measles 6
Germany 46
get dressed (to) 15
get lost (to) 50
get off (to) 39
get on (to) 39
get on well (to) 29
get up (to) 7, 15
ginger (hair) 3
girl 8
girlfriend 29
give (to) 22
give a hand (to) 17
glass 17
glasses 1, 6
gloves 2
go (to) 7, 20
go and see (to) 7, 22
go away (to) 7
go camping (to) 43
go down (to) 7
go for walks (to) 20
go home (to) 15
go in (to) 7
go near (to) 7
go out (to) 22
go past (to) 7
go swimming (to) 44
go through (to) 7, 26
go to bed (to) 15
go up (to) 7
goal 19
good 11, 28, 61
good evening 37
Good Friday 57
good luck 37
good morning 37
good night 37
goodbye 37
government 33
gramme 60
grandchildren 29
granddaughter 29
grandfather 29

grandmother 29
grandparents 29
grandson 29
grapes 16
grass 27
great 61
Great Britain 46
green 1, 62
green beans 16
greengrocer 18
grey 3, 62
grocer 10
grocer's 18
ground 19
ground floor 24
group 49
grow (to) 27
guide 49
guidebook 38
guitar 20
gymnastics 19

hair 3, 4
hairdresser 10
half 55, 60
ham 16
hand 4
handbag 2
handicrafts 30
handkerchief 2
hang up (to) 36
happen (to) 50
happy 11
happy birthday 37
happy New Year 37
harbour 25, 44
hard 61
hat 2
hate (to) 14
head 4
headache 6
headlines 21
headmaster 30
health 6
hear (to) 13

heart 4
heart attack 6
heart condition 6
heavy 61
hello 36, 37
help (to) 17
help! 52
hen 27
hesitate 14
hi! 37
high 61
highway code 51
hill 45
history 30, 58
hitch-hike (to) 43
hobby 20
hockey 19
hold on 36
hole 26
holiday 10, 49, 57
holidays 30
homework 15, 30
honest 11
hope (to) 14
hors d'oeuvre 16
horse 27
hospital 6
hospitality 49
hot 61
hotel 42
hour 55
house 24
housewife 17
housework 17
how much 18
however 34
hungry 5
hurry (to) 41
hurt (to) 6
hurt one's arm (to) 6
husband 8, 29
hygiene 17

ice 28
ice-cream 16

INDEX

idea 34
identity 8
identity card 38
if 34
ill 5, 6
immediately 55
immigrant 32
immobile 5
import (to) 33
important 10, 61
impossible 61
improve (to) 48
improvement 28
in 8
in front of 64
included 42
indicate (to) 34
industrial area 25
industry 10
inform (to) 34
information 39
inhabitant 25
injection 6
injured 51
injured person 51
insect 27
inside 24
instrument 20
insult (to) 11
insurance 26
insured 51
intelligent 11
intend (to) 10
Intercity train 39
interested in 10, 20
interesting 10, 20
international 33
interval 22
interview 21
introduce (to) 37
invitation 22
invite (to) 22
Ireland 46
Irish 47
iron 47
iron (to) 17

island 45
isn't it 34

jacket 2
jam 16
jeans 2
job 10
joint 16
journey 49
jump (to) 7, 19
jumper 2

key 24, 42
kill (to) 53
kilo 60
kilometre 60
kind (of) 61
kind (nice) 11
kind regards 35
king 33
kitchen 24
kitchen sink 24
knee 4, 7
knife 17
knitting 20
know (to) 29, 30
knowledge 30

lab(oratory) 30
lady 8
lake 45
Lake Constance 46
lamb 16
lamp 23, 24
landscape 27
language 30, 48
large 2
last 59
last (to) 58
late 39, 55
later 55
Latin 48
laugh (to) 12

launderette 18
lazy 11
lean (to) 7
learn (to) 30, 48
leather 63
leave (to) 10
lecturer 10
left 64
left luggage 39
left luggage lockers 39
left-wing 33
leg 4
lemon 16
lemonade 16
lend (to) 31
less 14, 60
let (to) (flat) 8
let (to) (allow) 11
letter 35
letterbox 24
level crossing 26, 39
library 30
lie down (to) 7
life 9
lift 24, 42
lift (to) 7
lift the receiver (to) 36
light 61, 62
lightning 28
like 14
like (to) 14
Lilo 43
line 41
list 38
listen (to) 13, 21
litre 60
little (a) 60
live (to) 8
live (to) (in place) 24
liver 4
liver pâté 16
living room 24
loan 31
local train 41

INDEX

London 46
long 2, 61
look (to) 1
look after (to) 17
look at (to) 13
look for (to) 10, 50
lorry 26
lose (to) (game) 19, 20
lose (to) (object) 50
lost property office 25
lot of 60
love 12
love (in letter) 35
love (to) 14
low 61
lower (to) 7
lozenge 6
luggage 39
luggage trolley 39
lunch 16
lying down 7

mad 11
Madam 8
magazine 20, 21
mail 35
main 25
main course 16
maintenance 26
make 26
make-up 3
man 8
manager 10, 42
many 60
map 25, 26, 41
market 18
married 8
marvellous 61
match (for fire) 16
match (sport) 19
maths 30
maybe 34
mayonnaise 16

mayor 33
meal 16
mean (to) 48
meat 16
mechanic 10
medicine 6
Mediterranean 46
medium 2
medium (meat) 16
meet (to) 50
meeting 10
melon 16
member 20
members of the family 29
membership card 43
mend (to) 17
menu 22
merry Christmas 37
metal 63
metre 60
middle 64
midnight 55
mild 28
mile 60
milk 16
milk jug 17
million 59
mineral water 16
minister 33
minute 55
mirror 23, 24
Miss 8, 65
miss (to) 39
mist 28
mistake 30
modern 61
modern languages 30, 48
moment 55
money 31
month 57
monument 25
moped 26
more 14, 60
morning 55

most 60
mother 29
motorbike 26
motorcyclist 26
motorway 26
mountain 45
mountains 27, 45
mouth 4
move (to) 7
Mr 8, 65
Mrs 8, 65
much 60
muggy 28
mum 29
Munich 46
Munich beer festival 49
museum 25
mushroom 16
music 20, 22, 30
musician 22
mustard 16
mutton 16

name 8
narrow 2, 61
national 33
natural 63
naturally 34
near 64
necessary 61
neck 4
need (to) 14
negotiations 33
neighbour 29
nephew 29
never 55
never mind 37
new 61
New Year's Day 57
New Year's Eve 55
news 21
news bulletin 21
newspaper 21
nice 11

INDEX

niece 29
night 42
nightclub 22
night porter 42
no (*answer*) 37
no (*not any*) 60
no parking 26
no (*answer*) 37
no (*not any*) 60
no parking 26
no thanks 37
no vacancies 42
nobody 8
noise 13
noisy 13
non-smoking 39, 40
noon 55
normal 61
north 64
North Germany 46
North Sea 46
Northern Ireland 46
nose 4
note (*money*) 31
nothing 60
notice (*to*) 13
now 55
number 8, 36
number plate 26
nurse 6, 10
nylon 63

O levels 30
occupation 10
offer (*to*) 22
office 10
often 55
oil 26
OK 34
old 1, 9, 61
oldest 29
omelette 16
on time 39
one way street 26
onion 16

only child 29
open 49
open (*to*) 7
opera 22
operation 6
operator 36
opinion 34
opinion poll 33
optician 18
optimistic 11
or 34
orange 16, 62
orchestra 22
order (*to*) 22
other 50
outing 20
outside 24
overcast 28
overcoat 2

package holiday 48
page 20
pain 6
paint (*to*) 20
pair 2, 60
pancake 16
pants 2
paper 35, 63
parcel 35
parents 29
park 25
park (*to*) 26
parking 26
party 22
party (*political*) 33
pass (*to*) 30
passenger 39, 40
passport 38
past 58
pastime 20
pastry 16
patient 6
patient (*ill person*) 61
pattern 20
pavement 26

pay (*to*) 10, 18, 31
pay back (*to*) 31
pay rise 10
payment 31
PE 30
peach 16
pear 16
peas 16
pedestrian 26
pedestrian crossing
26
pen 35
pencil 30, 35
penfriend 35
people 29
pepper 16
perfect 61
perfume 3
permission 11
person 8
pessimistic 11
pet 27
petrol 26
petrol pump attendant
26
petrol station 26
phone 36
phone (*to*) 36
phone book 36
phone box 36
phone call 36
photograph 20, 23
photography 20
physics 30
piano 20, 24
picnic 16
picture 24
picturesque 49
piece 60
pig 27
pill 6
pillow 15
pilot 40
pineapple 16
pipe 16
pitch 19

INDEX

pity 37
place 25
place of residence 8
plane 40
plant 27
plastic 63
plate 17
platform 39
play 22
play (to) 15, 19, 20
player 19
pleasant 11, 28, 61
please 37
pleased 11
pleased to meet you 37
plug 24
plumber 10
pocket 2
pocket money 31
point (to) 64
police 51
police station 53
policeman 10, 53
polite 11
politics 33
poor 31
pop music 20
pork 16
porter 39
possible 61
post (to) 35
post office 35
postage 35
postbox 35
postcard 35
postcode 8
poste restante 35
poster 23, 24
postman 10
potato 16
pound 31
prefer (to) 14
prepare (to) 17
prescription 6
present (gift) 22

present (time) 58
presently 55
president 33
press 21
pressure 26
pretty 1, 61
prevent (to) 11
price 18
price per day 42
primary school 30
prime minister 33
private 43
prize 30
problem 30, 32
profession 10
programme 21, 22
progress 30
promise (to) 34
pronounce (to) 48
protest (to) 32
Protestant 8
proud 11
prove (to) 53
provisions 18
pub 22
public opinion 33
public transport 41
pull (to) 7
pupil 30
purse 31
push (to) 7
put (to) 7
put down (to) 7
put on (to) 2
pyjamas 2
Pyrenees 46

quantity 60
quarter 55, 60
queen 33
question 30

rabbit 27
radiator 24, 26

radio 21
radio alarm 23
radio set 21
railway 39
rain 28
rain (to) 28
raincoat 2
rainy 28
raise the alarm (to) 52
rare 60
rare (meat) 16
raspberry 16
rather 1, 61
razor 3
read (to) 15, 20, 48
reading 20
really 34
receipt 18
receive (to) 35
reception 42
receptionist 42
recognize (to) 34, 50
recommend (to) 22
record 24
record player 24
red 62
Red Cross 52
red traffic light 26
reduced 18
reduction 18
redundancy 10
region 45
registered mail 35
reject (to) 10
religion 8
remain (to) 7
remove (to) 7
rent 24
rent (to) 8, 38
rental 26
repair (to) 26
repeat (to) 48
reply (to) 35
report 51
resort 49

INDEX

rest 7, 15
restaurant 22
result 30
return 7
return (to) 7
return ticket 39
reward 50
Rhine 46
Rhineland 46
rib 4
rice 16
rich 31
right 34, 64
right of way 26
right-wing 33
ring (to) 36
risk 54
river 45
road 26
road map 26
roadworks 26
roll 16
room 24, 42
rose 27
round 61
rubbish bin 43
rucksack 38
rugby 19
run (to) 7, 19

sad 11
salad 16
salary 10
sales 18
salt 16
salty 16
sand 44
sandals 2
sandwich 16
sanitary towel 6
sardine 16
saucepan 17
sausage 16
save (to) 31
savoury 16

say (to) 34
scarcely 60
school 30
science 30
scooter 26
score (to) 19
Scotland 46
Scottish 47
sculpture 20
sea 44, 45
seafood 16
seasick 6
seaside 44
season 57
season ticket 41
seat 39
seat belt 26
second 55
second class 39
secondary school 30
secretary 10
see (to) 13
see you later 37
see you soon 37
see you tomorrow 37
seem (to) 1
self-catering 49
self-service 18
sell (to) 18
send (to) 35
send for (to) 6
senses 13
sentence 35
separated 8
serial 21
serious 6, 11, 51
serve (to) 19
service 42
service included 22
set the table (to) 17
several 60
sew (to) 17
sex 8
shade 28
shampoo 3
shape 61

shave (to) 3
sheep 27
sheet 15
shirt 2
shoe 2
shoe size 2
shop 18
shop assistant 10, 18
shop window 18
shopkeeper 10
shopping 18
short 2, 61
shorts 2
shoulder 4
shout (to) 34
show 22
show (to) 64
shower 15, 24, 43
shower (rain) 28
showing 22
shy 11
sick 5, 6
sight 13
sign (to) 8
signature 8
silent 13
silly 11
simple 61
singer 10
singing 20
single 8
single ticket 39
sink (to) 44
sister 29
sit an exam (to) 30
sit down (to) 7
site 43
sitting 7
sitting room 24
situated 24
situation 10
size 2
ski 19
skiing 19
skin 4
skirt 2

INDEX

sky 28
sleep (to) 15
sleeping bag 43
sleeping berth 39
sleepy 5
slice 60
slim 1
slope 19
slot 35
slow 26
slow down (to) 26
slowly 48
small 1, 2, 61
small change 31
smell 13
smell (to) 13
smile (to) 7
smoke (to) 16
smoking 39, 40
smuggle (to) 38
snake 27
snow 28
snow (to) 28
soap 15
social 10
social security 10
Socialism 33
socialist 33
socks 2
sofa 24
soft 61
solid 61
something 18
son 29
song 20
soon 55
sore stomach 6
sore throat 6
sorry 11, 12, 37
sound 13
soup 16
south 64
South Germany 46
souvenir 49
Spanish 47
spare wheel 26

speak (to) 34, 48
speaking (on phone) 36
speciality 49
spell (to) 8
spend (to) 18, 31
spill (to) 50
spoon 17
spoonful 60
sport 19
sportsman 19
sportswoman 19
spot 1
sprain (to) 6
spring 57
spying 53
square (in town) 25
square (shape) 61
stadium 19
stairs 24
stamp 35
stand up (to) 7
standing 7
star 45
star (film) 22
start (to) 7
starter 16
state 33
station 39
stay 49
stay (to) 7
steak 16
steal (to) 53
stereo 24
stewardess 10, 40
sticking plaster 6
stockings 2
stomach 4
stop 39, 41
stop (to) 41
storm 28
straight ahead 64
strange 11, 61
strawberry 16
street 25
strike 10

strip cartoon 20
strong 5
student 30
study (to) 10, 30
stupid 11
subject 30
substance 63
subtitles 22
suburbs 25
successful 10
sugar 16
suit 2
suit (to) 2
suitcase 38, 39
summer 57
summer holidays 30
summit 45
sun 28
sunbathe (to) 44
sunburn 6
sunny 28
sunny interval 28
sunshine 28
sunstroke 6
supermarket 18
suppose (to) 34
sure 11
surgery 6
surprise 50
surprising 61
sweater 2
sweep (to) 17
sweets 16
swim (to) 19, 44
swimming 19
swimming costume 2
swimming pool 19
Swiss 47
switch on (to) 21
Switzerland 46

table 24
tablet 6
take (to) 7, 39
take-away 22

INDEX

take part in (*to*) 20
taken 39
tall 1, 61
tap 24
tape-recorder 24
tart 16
taste 13, 16
taste (*to*) 13
taxi 41
tea 16
teacher 10, 30
teaching 30
team 19
teenager 9
telegram 35
television 21
television news 21
tell (*to*) (*story*) 34
temperature
  (*illness*) 6
temperature
  (*weather*) 28
temporary job 10
tennis 19
tent 43
terrific 11, 61
Thames 46
thank (*to*) 37
thank you 37
thank you very much 37
thanks to 34
theatre 22
then 55
thief 53
thin 1, 61
thing 61
think (*to*) 32
thirsty 5
thousand 59
threaten (*to*) 53
throat 4
through train 39
throw (*to*) 19
throw away (*to*) 17
thunder 28

thunderstorm 28
ticket 39, 41
ticket office 39
tidy up (*to*) 17
tie 2
tight 2
tights 2
till 18
time 20, 58
timetable (*school*) 30
timetable (*train*) 39
tip 42
tired 5
title 20
to 39, 41
tobacco 16
tobacconist's 18
today 56
today's special (*dish*)
  16
together 22
toilet 24, 39, 42, 43
toilet water 3
toll 26
tomato 16
tomorrow 56
tongue 4
too 1
too much/many 60
tooth 4
toothache 6
toothbrush 15
toothpaste 15
totally 5
touch (*to*) 7, 13
tourism 49
tourist 49
tourist information
  bureau 49
tourist office 49
towel 15
town 25
town hall 25
toy 20, 23
track (*running*) 19
track (*train*) 39

trade 10
trade union 10
traffic 26
traffic lights 26
train 39
training 10
transistor 24
translate (*to*) 48
travel (*to*) 49
travel agency 38
travel agent's 18
traveller's cheque 31,
  38
tray 17
tree 27
trousers 2
trout 16
true 34
try on (*to*) 2
turn (*to*) 64
turn round (*to*) 7
two-star petrol 26
typist 10
tyre 26

ugly 1, 61
umbrella 2
uncle 29
under 64
underground 41
understand (*to*) 48
undoubtedly 34
undress (*to*) 15
unemployed 10
unemployed person
  10
unemployment 32
unfortunately 50
unhappy 11
United Kingdom 46
United States 46
university 30
unwell 6
upstairs 24
use (*to*) 17

INDEX

useful   10, 61
useless   61
usherette   10, 22
usually   15

vacuum (to)   17
vacuum cleaner   17
valley   45
vanilla   16
varied   61
VAT   42
veal   16
vegetable   16
vehicle   26
very   1, 61
video recorder   21, 24
Vienna   46
view   42
village   45
violence   32
visibility   51
visit   49
visit (to)   49
voice   13
vomit (to)   6

wage   10
wait (to)   41
waiter   10, 22
waiting room   39
waitress   10, 22
wake up (to)   15
Wales   46
walk   7, 20
walk (to)   7
wall   24
wallet   31
wallpaper   23, 24
want (to)   14

war   32, 52
wardrobe   23, 24
warm   28
wash (to)   15, 17
washbasin   24, 42
washing   17
washing machine   17
washing-up   17
watch   2, 55
watch (to)   21
watch out   37, 50
water   16, 63
weak   5
wear (to)   2
weather   28
weather forecast   28
week   56
weekend   56
weekly magazine   21
welcome   37
well   6, 61
well done (meat)   16
Welsh   47
west   64
western   22
West Germany   46
wet   61
when   55, 58
where   64
white   62
Whitsun   57
who   36
why   32
wide   2
widow   8
widower   8
wife   8, 29
win (to)   19, 20
wind   28
window   24
wine   16

winter   57
winter sports   19
wipe (to)   17
wish (to)   14, 37
with   34, 42
without   34
witness   51
woman   8, 29
wood   27
wool   63
word   35
work   10
work (to)   10
working class   33
workshop   10
world   45
worried   12
worry (to)   12
worse   61
write (to)   35
writing paper   35

X-ray   6

year   9, 57
yellow   62
yes   37
yes please   37
yesterday   56
yoghurt   16
young   1, 9
young girl   9
young man   9
youth hostel   43

zero   59
zip   2